School inclusion

The school, the family and the community

Mog Ball

© Joseph Rowntree Foundation

All rights reserved

Published by
Joseph Rowntree Foundation
The Homestead
40 Water End
York YO30 6WP

Tel: 01904 629241
Website: www.jrf.org.uk

ISBN 1 85935 041 0
Price £11.95

Designed by Adkins Design
Printed by Colorworks

Printed on recycled paper

JR
JOSEPH
ROWNTREE
FOUNDATION

Contents

1

Introduction

As a unit of social organisation the school presents an attractive foundation upon which to build. There are large numbers of them across the United Kingdom (22,165 in England in 1994/5), almost all children have to be in them for significant amounts of their time between the ages of 5 and 16, and they are recognised by the majority of the population, who have been to one themselves. Although much is made of the way schooling has changed, the basic ingredients - children, teachers, a building - remain familiar.

There has always been some elasticity to this familiar unit. Young people stay at school beyond the compulsory age of 16 years: roughly 70 per cent remain in full- or part-time education now, as compared to 50 per cent in 1980. Most children will be starting school younger: the Government has promised high quality education for all 4-year-olds whose parents want it, and an increasing amount of this will be provided by nursery units or classes in schools. A growing number of projects which enable children to arrive early in the morning and to remain after school hours are run on school premises or attached to schools.

The effectiveness of schools

What happens in the school has been focused in a National Curriculum in England and Wales. In Scotland pupils study a broad curriculum based on national guidelines. The testing of children against attainment targets forming part of this National Curriculum at 7, 11, 14 and 16 gives a measure of pupil academic achievement. The introduction of baseline assessment of children as they enter

school will mean, according to the Department for Education and Employment's White Paper *Excellence in Schools,* that:

> *"it will be possible to measure any pupil's progress through his or her school career, and also compare that pupil with any other individual or group, whether locally or nationally."*

The correlation of these results combined with external inspection by OFSTED provide a publicly available 'picture' of the progress of the school itself. Every school is inspected by OFSTED at least once every six years, more frequently where weaknesses are apparent. (Three hundred schools in England have been identified by OFSTED as failing to deliver an acceptable education.) Inspections review the support, guidance and welfare provision for pupils in the school, and also examine the links it has with parents and the community, though reports often cover the latter very briefly. This process has informed two key areas of enquiry: what makes a school 'effective', that is, able to ensure that the individual children in it reach the attainment targets within the National Curriculum? How can schools which are not 'effective' be improved?

The National Commission on Education, reporting in 1993, identified educational under-achievement in areas of high social stress as an acute problem.[1] As a result of an OFSTED Report on one of these areas - urban education - evidence of the nature of this stress was collected in a research paper which noted that low-income families were increasingly concentrated in particular neighbourhoods, especially peripheral council estates. Between 1979 and 1992 the percentage of children living in families where there was no full-time worker increased from 18 per cent to 30 per cent and the number of children on free school meals rose by 40 per cent between 1988 and 1993. DSS figures for 1993 showed that one in four children under 16 was living in a household on Income Support and that most of these children were young, almost 60 per cent being under 10.[2] A later study, of four urban communities, showed an increased spiral of deprivation, with residents pressured by crime and social breakdown, and with socially disruptive behaviour, particularly by young people, difficult to control. Unemployment rates were high on these estates, truancy rates in schools were much higher than average and four times more young people left school with no qualifications than the local authority average used by the study.[3]

But the idea that school success, in individual and collective terms, is attainable in the most inauspicious settings, has been a central tenet of education policy. Her Majesty's Inspectorate (HMI) has stressed repeatedly that social disadvantage is not an excuse for low expectations and poor teaching, and that a culture of low expectation, accepted by both family, community and school, must be combated.[4] The features listed in the OFSTED Framework for Inspection which are considered to lead to a school's improvement cover internal matters, particularly to do with classroom practice. However, among the 'key characteristics of effective schools' are two which can be construed, at least to a degree, as looking outwards towards the family and the community: high expectations among teachers, pupils and parents, leading to self-esteem and a stimulating level of challenge, and the nurturing of home-school partnerships that are founded on the belief that the support of parents has a positive effect on pupils' achievement.[5]

Statutory links between school and community

The management structure of schools offers opportunities to develop links with the family and the community. The control of school financing and budgets is delegated by Local Education Authorities (LEAs) to the governing bodies of schools. The composition of these bodies is defined by statute and will always include elected representatives of the parents of children in the school - between one and five people depending on the size of the school - and other representatives from the community, either appointed by LEAs, or co-opted by the governing body. It acts as a formal link between the local community and the school, and is required to produce a report each year summarising the progress and condition of the school. This is circulated to parents and an opportunity for comment on it must be made available. Parents can pass resolutions at this meeting, providing there are enough of them present.

The aims and policies of the school and the way standards of education can be improved are established by the headteacher and the governing body together. With the staff they will draw up the school development plan and help to decide how to spend the school's budget. Provided they fulfil their legal obligations they are constrained only in that the budget must be spent solely for the purposes of the school.

The school premises - buildings, land, equipment - are controlled by the governing body outside school hours, but the school is encouraged by statute to "be sympathetic to the needs of the local community when deciding out-of-hours use".[6] The law does not give specific control of how the premises of a maintained school are used during school hours to any particular body. Governing bodies therefore have some flexibility and can enter into agreements which allow the local community to use school buildings during school hours. However, they cannot use their budgets to subsidise non-school activities. They decide whether and how much to charge for the use of premises. LEAs can give directions to governing bodies about the use of premises, which do not remove the governing body's responsibility but cover matters like: regular bookings by the youth or adult education services; security and caretaking; what costs should be covered by charges; the use of a central booking system; and making sure that the community use of the school's facilities does not affect adversely the day-to-day use by pupils. Governing bodies have the power to enter into agreements allowing shared management of the premises so long as one of the aims is to encourage their use by the community.

Statutory support for children and families

The legislative framework for the provision of social support for children is embodied in the Children Act 1989. This brought together the public and private law relating to children, and recognised the rights of children to express views on decisions made about their lives, the rights of parents to exercise reponsibilities towards the child, and the duty of the state to intervene if and when the welfare of the child required. While recognising that the best place for children to be brought up is within their own family, the Act also acknowledges that families may experience difficulty in doing this, and that, in such cases, the local authority has a duty to intervene and help the parents to maintain or restore their ability to raise the child or children.

Local authorities have a general responsibility to promote the welfare of all children from 0-18 and specific duties towards children 'in need', a category widely defined by the Act in order to emphasise the kind of support which will prevent the need to intervene in families. This emphasis has been reinforced by a number of subsequent reports.[7] Local authorities themselves decide the categories of need, identify the children within them and assemble the services to support them. Social services departments take the lead in this process, in consultation with other agencies which work with families: health commissions and trusts, education authorities, the police and voluntary organisations. Since March 1996 it has been mandatory to publish a plan for the delivery of services to children, and to consult on this, including with parents.

There is a great variation in the ways in which local authorities define children in need.[8] In the past most have begun with those groups of children with whom they are already in contact - children 'at risk', 'looked after' and involved in the criminal justice system. Others add to this children in a variety of pre-determined groups, including disabled children, those with special educational or special health needs; young people at risk of criminal acts or in the penal system; children with difficult family relationships; those at risk of, or with HIV/AIDS; those in families which are homeless, in bed and breakfast accommodation, in sub-standard housing or where utilities have been cut off; where parents are unemployed, lone or divorcing; children cared for by disabled or mentally ill people; excluded from school or truanting; children misusing drugs or solvents; children from minority ethnic groups, including refugee children and those with English as a second language; children of travellers; from specific geographic areas, (often the peripheral estates mentioned above); and living in families with low incomes.

Social support and the school

Children identified as 'in need' are also, generally, in school. One of the ways of measuring whether their needs are being met is in the progress they make towards standard levels of achievement in school. This progress will depend heavily on the support they and their families receive to enable them to reach these levels. In identifying factors which contribute to pupil achievement in schools, a recent study of "effective schools in disadvantaged areas" noted the key role that parents played in enhancing the achievement of their children. Parents are defined as 'co-educators' (with the school) and 'co-learners' (with the child).[9] The 1997 Government White Paper on education notes, "We want to encourage more effective involvement of family learning in early years and primary education".[10]

There is considerable pressure for schools to enter into partnership with families, then, in order to help children to achieve within the school. But the involvement of 'outsiders' raises issues for clearly defined institutions like schools. If they are in contact with the whole family, will not areas of family need previously considered beyond the aegis of the school become an inevitable part of the school's concern? For example, if the school is encouraging parents to read with children, and the parents themselves are unable to read, the school will be directly concerned about a need within the family. In the past there was a tendency for schools and families to pass blame from one to another for shortfalls in the effectiveness of education. But if schools are to work in partnership with families, both will be required to address problems rather than to pass them on, and this suggests that there will be growth in the extent and types of relationships that schools will have with families and other agencies in the community.

The research study

In order to examine the current state of these relationships, a research project to study links between schools, families and communities in the UK was conducted between July and December 1997. Information was collected through searches of literature and information systems and through interviews with key personnel in a wide variety of agencies, from government and local government departments, national and local organisations and, occasionally, from individual schools. But the intention was to provide a broad overview of the field and signposts to what is happening rather than detailed information about specific practice.

The framework for this report on the research study assumes that education is a cumulative process, and that the story begins in the early years and proceeds chronologically. For the purposes of the study no distinction was made between private (fee-paying), grant-maintained and maintained schools. There is a significant difference, however, between the type of links with family and community undertaken by nursery, primary and secondary schools. As children grow older their need to be seen as autonomous increases, and the nature of the relationship between them, their families and services changes. For this reason the report takes a child-centred view, looking at what supports children to become happy, functioning young people and adults, as well as what contributes to the effectiveness of schools.

It was Aristotle who observed that, "there are useful things in which the young must be educated, like reading and writing, not only because they are useful but because they are often the means of learning yet further subjects," but we expect more of education in a modern democracy. To be completely successful it must develop in citizens what the philosophy of education calls 'civic virtues': dispositions towards justice, tolerance and honesty, trust and decency built on self-respect and self-esteem. As well as helping pupils to understand such dispositions, school, family and community are concerned to foster them in the adults of the future.

2

Beginning in the early years

The evidence that good quality nursery education will have long-term effects on educational and social achievement, and make it less likely that the child will be involved in crime or unemployed in adulthood, comes from well-known studies conducted in the United States into the Headstart and High/Scope programmes.[11] The aim of these pre-school 'enrichment' programmes was to address educational under-achievement among children considered at risk for socio-economic reasons. The beneficial effects on individuals were evident 25 years after they had experienced the programmes, because, as the evaluation argued, the pre-school intervention increased motivation and performance in primary school, which had a subsequent impact on later school performance. As one primary head explained, "We can do so much more if they have had a good start." Key features of these pre-school programmes were:

- parental involvement in the children's learning;
- encouragement for initiative, responsibility for actions, a spirit of inquiry, independence and self-confidence among the children.

Parents and toddlers

Support for families during the early development of the child in the UK has been characterised by diversity. Health services have a central role, with family practitioners, practice nurses and health visitors in contact with all families and involved in screening children for disabilities. It is rare for family clinics to be held on school premises, though some rural schools report that this still happens. The most frequent model for contact between school and health visitor is as part of a multi-agency approach, targeting the special needs of children and young families, particularly those of children in need of protection. There are some examples of collaboration between this service and education, however, to encourage early learning practices in families. In Birmingham health visitors present parents of children aged 9 months with "the child's first book and a library membership ticket for the local library". This scheme, pioneered by the Leisure and Community Services Department in the city, "while not apparently directed at schools will have a huge educational pay-off in the years ahead," believes the Chief Education Officer.[12]

Health visitors report some contact with schools when:

- developing support for families where the parent is experiencing isolation or post-natal depression by setting up, supporting or linking with social groups for parents and toddlers;
- contributing to parent-craft classes;
- working with groups of parents on specific issues, like the prevention of accidents;
- identifying and supporting households where there are young carers.

Parent and toddler groups may meet on school premises. Many are very fragile groupings, and it is difficult to assess how many there are in the UK. The Pre-School Learning Alliance (PLA) have surveyed 316 affiliated groups, but there are far more. In one rural area with six affiliated groups there were at least three times as many groups meeting at least once a week. Most affiliated groups (86 per cent) use community premises, like village and church halls, but 7 per cent report using school premises. In a study of successful schools in disadvantaged areas, which looked at eleven schools in the UK, two were reported as having a mother and toddler group meeting in the school.[13] This relationship is more common in primary schools, but it is also reported in secondary schools, where pupils may be involved in voluntary work with the group, and is particularly common in schools which are designated as 'community colleges'.

Daycare and schools

Provision for the early years has been collectively known as 'daycare', but this terminology is being overtaken by 'early years education'. It is provided by statutory, voluntary and private sources, although direct statutory provision of day care for children under three is now rare, and local authorities tend to 'contract out' services, often to nationally based voluntary organisations. The local authority is required to plan what is available to meet the needs of families in the area, and to publish a review every three years. The review is a multi-agency undertaking, and in some areas it has been led by staff from the LEA. The social services department has been required to register and inspect all provision and to make information about it available to parents. This responsibility is to pass to LEAs.

The diversity of early years provision has resulted in a tradition of collaboration between voluntary and private providers and local authorities. These collaborations, often known as 'early years forums', were the forerunners of the Early Years Partnerships which are now required by the DfEE to draw up Early Years Development Plans in each local authority. The new partnerships involve representatives of schools, parents, private and voluntary providers, health authorities, employers and others.

Although all pre-school provision involves parents to some degree, it has been the philosophy of the pre-school playgroup movement, in particular, to involve parents in the management and day-to-day running of groups. Ten per cent of pre-school playgroups in the PLA survey report that they use school buildings. This type of provision, formerly considered appropriate for children aged from 3 to 5 years, is not as popular with parents as day nurseries and nursery classes attached to schools.[14] It has strong community development credentials, however, and is likely to remain a significant element in the early years picture, because it is considered appropriate by a proportion of parents, and may be the only provision available for 2- and 3-year-olds.

At the beginning of 1996, 76 per cent of 4-year-old children in England were attending primary and nursery schools. Besides parental preference, reasons for this include falling primary school rolls, which have made space available, and concern that children born in the summer spend a shorter period in school than those born at other times in the year, and under-achieve as a consequence.[15] The result has been tension between schools which want to enlarge their pre-school provision and local, community-based services.

The tension has been overcome where schools and pre-schools have developed formal and informal links. Among the advantages of such links are:

- a smoother transition to school for the child, with continuity of learning;
- familiar adults in both settings;
- liaison about individual development and needs and joint assessment of any special educational needs;
- effective use of resources and facilities, with a wider range of interesting things for pre-school children to do;
- better links with other agencies which support the family;
- mutual recognition of the value of different approaches;
- earlier contact between school and parents.[16]

Partnerships between schools and pre-schools
The following examples illustrate some of the ways schools and pre-schools have formed links:

- Three small primary schools in a rural area of East Anglia have entered into agreement with a local voluntary playgroup which is well supported by parents, to use the playgroup as the pre-school centre. The centre will take all 4-year-olds until the term of their fifth birthday, when they will be admitted to their local school. The pre-school benefits from keeping the 4-year-olds, and from closer involvement in curriculum development with the partner schools.

- A primary school in the South West which shares its site with a voluntary pre-school has agreed that 4-year-olds will be gradually introduced to the school until they attend full-time in the term of their fifth birthday. The school and pre-school are collaborating on a shared curriculum. Each child's capacity to participate in the scheme is assessed not only on age thresholds but individually, in consultation with parents. The shared site has been crucial in this development.

- A school with a purpose-built nursery facility, but no budget to open a nursery, entered into an agreement with a playgroup to rent the premises. Children started at the playgroup at 2 years and 10 months, and transferred to the primary school at 4 years and 6 months or when they were ready. When the LEA changed the admission date to primary schooling to 4 years, the playgroup's numbers were due to drop. To avoid closure the school has negotiated with the playgroup to purchase up to four sessions a week in the playgroup for all 4-year-olds in the reception class. This has met with the approval of parents, who wanted a flexible arrangement for their children that enabled them to spend time in school and playgroup according to their needs.

- An LEA employs specialist early years teachers to support schools and voluntary pre-school groups by:
  - providing good quality early years experiences for pre-school children;
  - providing a link between pre-school groups and local schools;
  - assisting children in the transition from pre-school to school by, for example, taking one or more children to visit their prospective school, or relieving a reception class teacher so that they can visit a pre-school group.[17]

The family centre approach

More comprehensive support for parents is provided by 'family centres', a label used for varied provision which, when fully realised, has the following characteristics:

- a commitment to work with both parents and children;
- a range of services for both children and adults;
- flexible work styles, to suit the needs of families and individuals;
- a neighbourhood base, from which most users are drawn;
- an emphasis on local involvement and participation by users;
- a community work or preventive approach;
- building on strengths and skills in the community rather than 'delivering services';
- aiming to increase the confidence and self-respect of users and to increase their skills and understanding of their children.[18]

Many family centres are run by nationally based children's voluntary organisations like the Children's Society, Barnardos and NCH Action for Children, in areas of acute disadvantage, often in partnership with the local authority. Efforts have been made in some areas to set up family centres attached to schools but the Family Centre Network has only two in its membership of over two hundred. It is likely that there are more: South Glamorgan County Council (now Vale of Glamorgan) reports the development of a network of family centres "the latest of which were integral to schools and unique in having social workers based in them, putting child protection at the heart of family support."[19]

Staff in some family centres report that they have been approached by local primary schools for help in coping with difficult behaviour in the classroom and in involving parents in their child's learning. The aim of empowering parents means that the family centre approach focuses on what parents can teach staff, who will need time to build the sort of relationships where this can happen. There is not enough time in most primary schools. In addition, the 'empowerment' approach requires sophisticated facilitating skills which are not a central part of the primary teacher's training or experience. One worker from a family centre who visited a school to help teachers with 'classroom control' found herself left with the disruptive classes, providing respite but not much development for the teacher.

Pre-school support for families with disabled children

Families with a child or children with special needs are likely to have some professional support, provided by statutory and voluntary agencies, throughout the pre-school period. Such families may have contact with a range of health professionals (paediatric nurses, speech, occupational and physio- therapists), and support from social workers and specialist voluntary agencies. The numbers can become a problem since each service often requires a separate assessment and a great deal of effort on the family's part before it is established. However, these difficulties are recognised by the agencies, and considerable effort is being made to improve co-ordination, both through the use of the Children's Services Plan and through projects set up by multi-agency groups.

These links with support agencies may continue as the child reaches school age and for many special schools they are an established part of the local network. Mainstream schools have been less accustomed to contact with specialist professionals, but the increasing integration of children with special needs is leading to the development of closer links with specialist services in some areas.

'Portage' is a model of pre-school education for disabled children which involves parents and has begun to influence practice in primary schools. It is designed to help parents to teach children at home. Portage teachers visit individual families on a weekly basis and identify new skills which parents would like the child to learn. Ways of teaching these skills are agreed, written down and demonstrated by the teacher, so that the parent is familiar with the teaching task before the home teacher leaves. Around 80 per cent of local authorities in England report a Portage service, and some counties have two or three. Over half are funded by LEAs only, but there are many examples of multi-agency funding partnerships which may involve education with health, social services and the voluntary sector.

The Portage model has wider applicability and developments based upon it include a special parenting service for parents with moderate learning difficulties, and school-based outreach work. It has allowed home teachers from a wide variety of professional and non-professional backgrounds (many are volunteer parents who have benefited from the programme) to support parents in teaching their children everyday skills and helping them to manage disruptive or inappropriate behaviour. "Most of all, it enabled parents to take a renewed pride in their child's progress and development."[20]

Pre-school home links

Many primary schools try to make links with individual families through home visits by reception teachers before a child starts school. In Scotland, outreach programmes where parents are visited at home are facilitated by community educators. In some areas visits begin as soon as the child is enrolled in the primary school, and community education and school staff make contact and talk about the school. These first visits are followed by pre-entry workshops,

jointly led again, which introduce parents to the teaching methods used in the school, and reassure them - and the children - about the activities they will encounter in the classroom.[21]

> **Preparing the pre-school child and family**
>
> A 'model' programme, called Parents as Teachers (PAT) and developed in the United States, was first introduced into the UK by a primary head in Buckinghamshire who had trained as a 'parent educator' in Missouri. The school-based programme brings together parents of children from birth to 3 years to explore parenting, child development and early learning. The parent counsellors who lead these groups may be teachers from the school or others, including parents, who have undergone the training.

If pre-school children are beginning to show signs of developmental, emotional or behavioural disturbance, the transition to school can prove traumatic and the difficulties may increase. Fifty per cent of children exhibiting these disturbances first begin to present them after starting at primary school.

> **Working with families where children have behavioural problems**
>
> Another American model, developed in Seattle, is aimed at families where the pre-school child is showing signs of developmental, emotional or behavioural disturbance of clinical severity, which can undermine successful transition to school. A pilot project in Oxford is working with a maximum of ten families, who are referred by health visitors, social workers, schools and other agencies. The project employs specialist workers who teach parents a set of principles and skills about praise and play, how to set limits, how to deal with misbehaviour without harshness and how to develop communication and problem-solving within the family.[22]

Parent education programmes work with families of primary-age as well as pre-school children. They have burgeoned rapidly and are not clearly differentiated in terms of aims, styles and methods. In one local authority there are eighteen different programmes, and this may not be unusual. A survey of 38 group-based parenting programmes in the UK found that written reports were available for less than half, and external evaluations for nine only.[23] The Parenting Forum, based at the National Children's Bureau, provides support and co-ordination, and is working on guidelines for various aspects of these programmes.

The rapid expansion of parenting support at pre-school and school entry will require systematic monitoring and examination on more than a project-by-project basis. There has been concern that some 'model' programmes, developed overseas and imported to the UK, may be inappropriate for cultural and other reasons. There is also a diversity of approach - length of course, methodology, numbers of parents and many others - which suggest that this is an area where careful scrutiny will be necessary.

In the comprehensive long-term project, described below, such scrutiny is integrated in the design. The overall programme is interesting in that it offers continuity and progression from birth into the school experience, based upon:

- opportunities to learn;
- recognition of achievement;
- interactions with adults in learning situations;
- models of literacy and numeracy behaviour, learning strategies and dispositions.[24]

A secondary school has been a prime mover in this example. It expects to benefit from the impact of the project when the children reach secondary age.

A pre-school family support programme

This significant project has emerged from a secondary school working with the LEA, the local university and a prominent member of the business community in Oxfordshire. It is funded by central government and local government through the Single Regeneration Budget (SRB), charitable trusts and local businesses.

There are seven first schools and three middle schools in the area. The pre-school programme, known as PEEP, began in 1995 and will last for five years in the first instance. The key principle is that all children in the defined geographic area - a peripheral estate - are eligible to take part in the programme and that as many as possible will be involved in it over the five years. This amounts to large numbers of children. There will be 100 new babies and 100 3-year-olds in the area each term. By 1998-99 it is expected that 1,300 children will be participating.

The curriculum for this programme is divided into three parts, the first two for children from 0-3 and 3 -5, pre-school and in transition, and the third for children from 5 to 7 who have entered school. Each child has a Child Learning Record which contains a record of activities, progress and advice and support appropriate to the child's age, which aims to give child and family a sense of progress and achievement. Every child, with parent or carer, attends a weekly group session with ten or twelve others, led by a pair of trained leaders. Groups and leaders stay together throughout the project, for mutual support and to build trust, and to share stories, rhymes, songs, books and other learning experiences.

There are many other features to this ambitious project, but one which overlaps with the school is the After School Story Time, which occurs in each first school once a term for 40 minutes and is open to all Reception and Year 1 children, teachers and parents. These sessions offer an activity to children who are over the age for involvement in the project, give parents a chance to participate, and reinforce the links between the pre-school project and school staff.[25]

Summary

All primary schools have a general relationship with families of children due to enter the reception class, which involves the exchange of information, visits by parents and child to the school, and, in some areas, visits to the home by teachers or specialist home/school link staff. Closer relationships evolve if:

- there is a *structural relationship* with pre-school provision based on:
  - shared buildings;
  - shared staff;
  - formal agreements with specific pre-school facilities.

- the school takes a role in *empowering parents* by using family centre, Portage or other approaches to preparing the child for school, which boost parental confidence and ability to participate;

- there are *targeted programmes* to reach families where a deficit in the social or physical development of the child has been identified before the child starts at school;

- there are *support programmes* geared to providing parents with skills, especially to manage behaviour, which they may feel they lack;

- targeted and support programmes draw on the expertise of staff from *local specialist agencies,* like health visitors, speech therapists, voluntary organisations, and from the school itself;

- availability of targeted and support programmes *continues* once the child has entered primary school.

3

Inside and outside the primary school

Primary education in England is carried out in a variety of schools. Infants schools take children up to 7. First schools educate them from 5 to 10, junior schools from 7 to 11, middle schools from 8 to 13. In Scotland, primary schools largely cater for children from 5 to 11, and in Northern Ireland from 4 to 11.

Involving the family

There has been a good deal of research showing that good home-school links result in better individual achievement and better behaviour in the school.[26] Evidence from a comparative study in Haringey of improving children's reading showed that in those projects where parents were involved, children made most progress. Participation by parents has been consistently reinforced by major reports on education since the early sixties, including the Warnock Report in 1978: "the successful education of children with special educational needs is dependent on the full involvement of their parents."[27]

Some local authorities have established resources to support this relationship.

A borough-wide scheme to develop links with families

PACT (Parents, Children and Teachers), in Hackney, has a co-ordinator based in a Parents Centre who organises:

- projects for children, like home-school reading and maths, where parents and teachers collaborate to help children;
- projects for children and parents together, like family literacy groups and environmental days;
- projects for parents to learn skills, based in schools, and covering a range of learning, from pottery to child development.

The co-ordinator of Hackney PACT notes that "parents and teachers do not always collaborate with ease." Among difficulties he notes are a tendency for teachers to be over-defensive when challenged or criticised by parents; an inclination for teachers to dominate in meetings with parents; and a lack of skills and experience in interacting with parents. "Perhaps most significantly, teachers' working conditions allow little prime time for unhurried contacts with parents ... ."[28] The Chief Inspector of Education has also questioned the extent to which teachers have entered into partnership with parents.[29]

More common than the authority-wide co-ordination role is the location of home-school liaison staff within an individual school. Both types of post have been supported by a variety of funding initiatives with different aims. For example, projects jointly funded by the Department of the Environment and local authorities under the Single Regeneration Budget, City Challenge and the Urban Programme in Scotland have supported such posts with the aim of inner-city improvement. The DfEE and the Scottish Education

Department have funded them through GEST (Grants for Educational Support and Training) and the Improving Schools Initiative in order to raise standards in schools, improve school attendance and support children and young people from minority ethnic groups. Funding from the Home Office has paid for home-school liaison work to "strengthen ties between schools and the parents of ethnic minority pupils whose ties are hard to establish because of parents' lack of English or because of cultural or social factors, so as to enable parents to become more fully involved in the education of their children and in the work of the schools".[30] The Home Office has also funded posts for specialists to work with travellers and refugee families. Multi-agency partnerships like Education 2000 and central and local combinations of voluntary, statutory and private sector funding have contributed to posts based in schools, local government agencies and community organisations.

Increasing demand

Despite this plethora of development, charitable trusts report an increase in applications for funding to support the appointment of specialist home-school liaison staff in schools or in groups of schools.[31] This is reflected, too, by requests from community development projects for support by schools in some areas. It is difficult to generalise the purposes for which these posts are required, but the management of difficult behaviour and the increasing exclusion of children from the school are most frequently cited.

Specialist workers based in schools

Schools' Outreach, a voluntary organisation in the West Midlands which works with schools to recruit, train and support workers, known as 'pastoral care workers', for this role in both primary and secondary schools, notes the following aspects of the job:

- collaboration with the Education Welfare Officer to improve attendance at school;
- classroom support for individual children experiencing difficulties in class;
- strategies to reduce and counter bullying through group and individual work with bullies and victims, counselling of parents, support for staff in dealing with bullying and interventions in conflicts;
- drama workshops on managing conflict and anger;
- group and individual work to improve self-esteem, communication and to build a 'caring environment';
- individual home visits to improve links with parents;
- running facilities in the school to encourage parental participation (including provision of crèche facilities);
- liaising with other agencies in the area: Parish and District councils over play and recreation provision, health centres, social services departments, child guidance services and voluntary agencies.

In an evaluation for the LEA of such a post in a primary school, the headteacher noted: "Our worker has enabled us to take the children off-site in small groups, support staff and pupils in so many ways and has reached out to parents in a friendly, supportive, non-threatening way which has dramatically increased their confidence in the school. A crucial component of her role is that of not being a teacher. A number of pupils with considerable tensions have confided in her, sought her advice and are prepared to listen." One of the performance indicators for this post was the rate of exclusions from the school, which had reduced from 50 temporary exclusions in the year before it began to one permanent and two temporary exclusions after the second year of the project. In addition the school had taken seven pupils who had been excluded or transferred from other schools.[32] Because it occurs on the spot, the approach of such workers combines preventive work and some intervention in crises.

Special educational needs co-ordination

It is estimated that up to 20 per cent of school children will need special educational support at some time during their school careers. This may mean extra help in class, or teaching provided by a special unit attached to the school or in a special school. The LEA is responsible for assessing children with the most severe and complex special educational needs (SEN) (about 3 per cent of the pupil population) and providing a statement for them. They are also responsible for arranging the provision that is necessary to meet the needs of these children.

Each school has a named teacher who is responsible for the day-to-day running of the school's SEN policy and who:

- advises teachers in the school;
- co-ordinates the teaching for children with SEN;
- maintains an SEN register and oversees the records of these children;
- liaises with families;
- contributes to the in-service training of staff;

- works with external agencies including the educational psychology service and other educational support, health, social services and the voluntary sector.

The parallel requirement for local authorities to keep a register of disabled children based on multi-agency collaboration has resulted in improved liaison between SEN co-ordinators (known as SENCOs) and local family support agencies in some areas. This has led to joint assessments of the needs of children joining a mainstream school which take into account the needs of the whole family, including siblings. An example of this process in action in a secondary school can be found on page 36.

The school as co-ordinator of support services

In the past it has been local authorities through their social services departments which have taken the lead in co-ordinating services for family support. They have the statutory responsibility, they take the lead role in children's services planning, and they have a long history of joint working with health and voluntary sector agencies. There are, however, a few interesting examples where it is a *school* which has co-ordinated the other agencies.

Co-ordination of services by the school (through a partner voluntary organisation)
The National Pyramid Trust is a voluntary organisation which supports class teachers in screening children, usually at 7 or 8, against a health and welfare checklist. This covers the child's progress in school, attendance and punctuality, physical development and well-being, interest and personal adjustment. The list, completed by the teacher, is described as a help for teachers to "organise their thoughts, as the first step towards initiating action. The next

stage will be a systematic attempt by your school, working with parents and support agencies, to devise a preventive strategy for each child that has been identified."[33]

Schools arrange a multi-disciplinary meeting for all health and welfare staff attached to the school: educational psychologist, education welfare officer, school nurse, child guidance, etc., where the class teacher of the year group in question presents the concerns that have emerged from the screening. These meetings identify at least one positive intervention for each child discussed: counselling for parents, a special medical examination, a change in the child's academic or social curriculum or an additional activity.

The Pyramid Trust offers after-school activity groups for ten children with three trained adult volunteers to promote self-esteem, resilience and maturity among the children. "The groups are run as the children's own 'gang' or secret society that offers every child a chance to be accepted and belong. They choose their own name, activities and even set the rules."[34]

This approach has been used in three local authorities in London and Wales and the progress of a small group of participating children has been the subject of a short-term evaluation.

The logical extension of school co-ordination is the location of other agencies within or attached to schools. This model has been developed in parts of the United States where poor populations need support from a range of services, including housing and benefit advice as well as social and health support. It is based on a close relationship between the school and the family, and only works if families are happy to visit schools and feel comfortable in them.[35] Thus it may also be a logical extension of the kind of home-school links and family support that is being developed in the UK.

There are vestiges of this approach. Some Children's Services Plans examine the idea of the school as a central point for service delivery to families - the 'complete school' it is called in one authority. But as yet there is little evidence of full-scale development, except in the following example.

The 'full-service' school

Manchester City Council has begun a pilot project which aims to support children and families through schools so that they reach a situation where their need for education and health care support approximates to the general demand, without additional services. Long-term support will be available where difficulties continue, or require regular services - for disabled children and their families, for example.[36]

Collaboration between a large number of agencies is apparent at every level of this pilot programme. Besides the customary health, education, social services and voluntary sector participation, overall planning includes housing, probation and police contributions. "This serves two functions: it commits the services concerned to ensure that the relevant field workers are available to take part in project work and ensures that decisions can be taken within the group that can actually change practice."[37]

The scheme is co-ordinated by a headteacher who has been seconded by the education department. The three primary schools chosen for the pilot projects have all had experience of multi-agency work and have a community or parents' room. Each school has its own multi-agency support group, which always includes the co-ordinator and the school's head, social services team manager, education welfare officers, early years and play managers, health representatives - usually a school nurse - and representation from the parents, voluntary sector, community police and adult education. There is also a local community action group attached to each school, "to provide a structure through which access and take up of services can be addressed and encouraged".[38]

The project is still in its early stages, but the evaluation will provide insights into the 'full service' approach in the UK.

In Tower Hamlets another multi-agency project is in the first stages of development based in a secondary school, but also serving children from three local primary schools. Initially this 'children's centre' project will be funded by a charitable trust. It will be particularly interesting because it is for children of 8 to 14. These approaches are based on two hypotheses. The first, already alluded to, is that family support will reduce the need for interventions by the participating agencies, especially the social services departments. The second is that the projects will eventually contribute to a reduction in juvenile crime, although it is unlikely that locally based family support services alone can make an impact on its causes.

Summary

Primary schools are developing relationships with families and the community in three settings: the home, the school itself and the community. There is an argument that the latter is the most suitable setting for work with families where there has been a poor experience of school, and opportunities for contributions by volunteers and a wider range of specialists,

like community arts workers, are presented. However, individual schools are also developing family involvement programmes which draw on community-based approaches. Initiatives include:

- authority-wide projects, where support is offered to families *outside the school* but with the aim of improving the links between families and individual schools;

- projects within schools involving the appointment of *specialist staff* who work with all children but *target* those who are having behavioural or learning problems. There is evidence that more schools want such posts;

- *general family involvement programmes* often led by the PTA and offering a wide range of social activities for school staff, parents and children together;

- *learning enhancement programmes* involving parents and children together;

- *remedial skills programmes* addressing the learning needs of parents in literacy, numeracy and 'parenting skills', though the latter are often offered generally rather than targeted;

- providing a base for *family support services* in or attached to schools, to offer parents a 'one-stop' place to find help and professional staff ease of collaboration;

- the example provided by *SEN co-ordination* in schools and the plans to develop parent partnership schemes to enable parents of children with SEN to influence and contribute to their children's education, outlined in the 1997 DfEE

Green Paper *Excellence for all children: Meeting special educational needs* provides a blueprint for collaboration between schools, families and other agencies.

- *full-service* or *'re-structured' schools* which are used as a base by other family support agencies, both statutory and voluntary.

4

Growing up: support in middle childhood

It is widely acknowledged that sources of support for children in middle childhood are less developed than those for younger and older children.[39] This is the period when the balance between autonomy, the need to relate to other people and the need for supervision may vary from child to child. Some supervision is likely to be required, but the development of personal interests and skills should give the child a chance to pursue his or her own interests.

Too much supervision?

However, there has been a general trend in the recent past to increase levels of supervision for children in middle childhood. Bronfenbrenner has argued that many societal factors conspire to isolate children from the rest of society, including the fragmentation of the extended family, the separation of residential and business areas, occupational mobility, separate patterns of social life for different age groups and the delegation of childcare to specialists. Increased road traffic, which has added to the perceived threat to children and means that most are transported to school, has led to a rapid change, famously documented by the Policy Studies Institute.[40]

In addition, dangers to children, both in and out of school, have been highlighted by tragedies like that in Dunblane, and the developing awareness of child abuse and paedophilia. In response, schools have become extremely security conscious, and have been funded to be so by the

DfEE. Most have now secured their perimeters, can monitor visitors and limit their access to one entrance. Many have surveillance equipment and even security staff. Recommendations by the Cullen Inquiry will result in a system of accreditation to a national body of clubs and groups voluntarily attended by children and young persons under 16 years of age, for their recreation, education and development. The main purpose of this will be to make sure that leaders and workers undergo adequate police checks. Hitherto this requirement has applied only to organisations for children under 8 years. There has been no investigation of the impact such measures have on the development of autonomy in children of 8 to 14.[41]

Primary-secondary links

Links between primary and secondary schools offer opportunities to counteract this trend. They are becoming more common, although they are simultaneously more difficult to forge as parental choice means that the obvious link between 'feeder' primary schools and secondary schools has become more tenuous. In one urban authority a secondary school receives pupils from 71 primary schools. Though this is an extreme example, researchers recognise this tendency. It is less marked in rural areas where there is good evidence of links. In Essex, for example, there are 13 consortia with primary schools linked to a single secondary school; in Hereford and Worcester, four primary schools link with a secondary school in a 'pyramid'; in Suffolk it is one high school with ten primary schools, in Cambridgeshire eight are involved. The relationship involves activity days, liaison days, visits and co-operation between Parent Teacher Associations.[42]

Other activities which have brought together secondary and primary children include:

- one-to-one help with reading;
- help with sports coaching and tournaments;
- drama projects;
- presentations about bullying, safety and drugs (often using drama);
- 'buddy' schemes where primary pupils are paired with an older mentor from the secondary school, who supports them before, during and after the transition.

In Scotland home visits by community education staff can also occur at the transition stage from primary to secondary school. As a result some parents have volunteered to take part in educational programmes to help primary children settle into the new school. Setting aside a room for parents, which has become common in primary schools, is now happening in some secondary schools. Guidance to parents on helping with homework is now available through the Parent Prompts programme, which links with the 5 to 14 curriculum.[43]

Drugs education

The age-group has been targeted by a number of local projects which aim to prevent drug misuse using different approaches. Examples include:

- visits by 9- to 11-year-olds to classrooms at the stadia of local Rugby League Clubs in Bradford, where sports personalities contribute as role-models in sessions on drugs education, health promotion and the development of self-esteem;

- theatre-in-education presentations to 10- and 11-year-olds in Brent, to raise awareness of drugs and drug-related issues, raise self-esteem and promote resistance to peer pressure, combined with training for school governors, a family support programme, a hotline for parents and curriculum support;

- Drug Abuse Resistance Education (DARE), a 17-week course for 9- to 11-year-olds delivered by police officers in Kirklees, combined with Parents as Educators (PAE), a programme bringing parents and children together to share the experience of learning about drugs, so that children receive the same information from school and home;[44]

- Chemical Abuse Resolution Lies in Education (Project Charlie) implemented since 1990 for 8- to 12-year-olds in Hackney, and aiming to promote abstinence from drugs, to delay the onset of experimentation with drugs, to limit eventual drug use and to inhibit the development of drug use among this group.[45]

Research needed

There is a need for more information about the sources of support required by children in this age-group. There is evidence of some regression in learning after the transfer to secondary education, and truancy and other 'at risk' behaviour are often rooted in the transition period. Research by educational psychologists in the United States suggests that help at this age is most effective when part of a network that includes peers, pets, parents, hobbies and environmental sources of support. Importantly, participation in informal, unsponsored meeting places and unstructured opportunities to get away by oneself actually help children to develop a social perspective. Organisations that allow the child to experience autonomy and to master the content of an activity are most appropriate, and work better than formal organisations and structured activities. But improving informal sources of support for children in middle childhood will mean listening very carefully to children and having regard to their perspective.

Summary

The projects for children in this age-group:

- are likely to be based on *preventive education* to influence personal development and attitudes to sexual behaviour, drug use and criminal activity;

- indicate the need for *intensive programmes*, the *involvement of parents* and the importance of *continuing the approach* into secondary school;

- may draw on *peer tutoring* methods, where older students work, often on a one-to-one basis with younger pupils;

- often involve *the police force*, which contributes to preventive education and to diversionary activities, like play and outdoor pursuits for young people considered 'at risk';

- may work with the Articles of the United Nations Convention on the Rights of the Child to support children in *finding a voice* to express their views and preferences;

- bring the school into contact with *leisure and recreation departments* in district councils, *voluntary organisations* providing activities, (including sports, arts, and interest-based activities);

- need to pay particular attention to *child protection issues*.

5

Secondary schools and partner agencies

The personal and social development of young people is a central concern for youth work. This discipline has traditionally complemented formal education but also works on its own terms for independent purposes, which do not use the same apparatus as schools to judge effectiveness. The youth service offers activities which are not compulsory, in contrast to school. Fewer youth workers are now employed by local authorities, with more working for national and local specialist voluntary agencies. They support young people as they make decisions concerning their lives and responsibilities, including the transition from school to training and employment. The priority age range for youth work is generally seen to be 14 to 19 years. "The range of styles of youth work may encompass group work, individual counselling and advice, residential experiences, outreach and detached work and mobile youth projects, many of which can and have taken place from school-based settings."[46]

Youth work in schools

Voluntary youth organisations of all sorts use schools as bases and conduct many activities in them - Duke of Edinburgh's Award, Scouts, Guides, Red Cross Cadets and countless others. But there is a tension between the role of the school as an institution and the needs of the young person as supported by the youth service that means there is a continuing debate about school-based youth work. Can it reach all young people, or will those who have problems in school be put off talking to youth workers if they are linked too closely to the school? If youth work is concentrated on young people 'in need', will the generality of young people want to have contact with it?

The National Youth Agency (NYA) lists only 47 general youth work projects directly based in schools, often in a youth centre attached to the school, and 45 projects aimed at young people 'at risk' of exclusion or non-attendance at school. (There are likely to be other projects which are not on the NYA list.) The latter are often based on a wider partnership with the Children's Services Plan agencies and other organisations like Training and Enterprise Councils (TECs), local crime reduction and prevention partnerships, careers and probation services.

The arguments for using the school as a base for youth work include the access this can give to superior facilities, the opportunities for day-to-day contact with young people and the chance to develop better inter-agency working, as well as closer relationships with teachers. In a paper on this subject the authors feel that both workers and schools benefit, and that youth workers are better able to understand the problems which schools pose for young people and "where appropriate, to seek to change the practices of schools and involve themselves in the reform of those situations".[47] However, in another publication the same authors note that 'informal educators' (a definition that includes youth workers) "have been encouraged to define themselves by saying what they are not.

And in the main they are not school teachers."[48] The key difference is the amount of control that a teacher can exert over where, how and what goes on, usually in a classroom, but more generally on the school premises. "Informal education is based around conversation: formal around curriculum."[49]

Young people needing help

It may be formal education that is creating the need for personal support among young people - the sort of help that youth workers offer. For example, a report in 1996 based on a study of over 1,000 children in 16 secondary schools showed that 79 per cent were more worried about examinations and school work than about anything else in their lives. Sixty-six per cent were also worried about their future. This study examined in depth the cases of almost 200 children who had called a national help-line because they were worried about their exams. Thirteen had contemplated suicide and one had attempted it. These callers were all at secondary school but a proportion had been there for a year or less.[50]

Exclusions from school have risen dramatically since 1990. Three types of exclusion were formalised by the 1986 Education Act: fixed term, indefinite and permanent. In 1990-91 the number of permanent exclusions from school was 2,910. In 1995-96 it was 12,476. A 1996 report found that this rise and the difficulty of finding alternative placements for excluded pupils was overwhelming some local authorities. Children are excluded from both primary and secondary schools, and the numbers have been rising in both, but exclusion is a far bigger issue for the secondary school. In 1995-6 the overall figure of 12,476 permanently excluded pupils included 1,608 from primary schools, 524 from special schools and 10,344 from secondary schools. Factors

making it more likely for a child to be excluded included gender - boys were more likely to be excluded than girls; ethnicity - African-Caribbean children were four times more likely to be excluded than other children; children with special educational needs - 17 per cent of the children in this year of the survey had statements of special educational need.[51]

It has been suggested that a reason for this rapid growth in the use of permanent exclusion has been that parental choice and the system of school 'league tables' has influenced school decisions to exclude pupils. The numbers of excluded children with special educational needs, especially emotional and behavioural difficulties, point to a need for closer relationships between schools and other agencies responsible for supporting such children - educational psychology, social services and voluntary sector specialist agencies.

Co-ordination of services to support young people and schools
In Wiltshire trained emotional and behavioural development co-ordinators have been attached to secondary schools to advise teachers on the management of difficult behaviour and to prevent problems from escalating to exclusion levels. Primary schools are offered support from a specialist based in local social services area teams, who can help the school find extra help from social services resource centres, perhaps, or child and family guidance services. In this area there is an acknowledgement that young people who present difficulties are sometimes passed from agency to agency and that the school may feel that it is at the end of the line and left to do a difficult job remote from sources of support. An 'adolescent support team' is being designed to provide support to "frontline staff in a range of settings, but especially in schools".[52]

In Kent an individual school has made a direct approach for help to a national, research-based institute which specialises in the needs of adolescents. The approach emerged from a request from parents of children in Year 8 at the school, 12- to 13-year-olds who are still in the 'transition' stage described in the previous section. The parents expressed a need for more support to help them cope with their children's behaviour. The school had already excluded six children in the first four weeks of term, and this was not a school which had lightly excluded children in the past. With support from the local authority, the institute will work intensively with all the parents of the children in this year, interviewing them, offering them a range of services on parenting, like workshops, audio-visual materials and, perhaps, a counsellor at the school. The idea is to pre-empt further behaviour problems in the school by targeting one year - a preventive approach but emerging from a crisis. It is hoped that this project will point the way to some cost-effective continued support for these parents.

Collaboration between agencies to help targeted young people

The Community Education Service in Cambridgeshire is divided into 20 local patches and has a long track record of collaboration with other local and national statutory agencies and voluntary organisations. Three 'patches' had special concerns about the behaviour of young people, within and outside school, which were shared with other agencies. Funding from the DfEE GEST programme enabled the service to develop work in these three areas, one of them a large local authority housing estate, originally built as 'London overspill' in the sixties. The community education work already going on in this 'patch' aimed to improve the self-esteem and social responsibility of 13- to 17-year-olds at risk of

criminal activity, to involve young people in developing the programme, to promote inter-agency collaboration and to contribute to crime prevention.[53]

The youth work with two schools has thus taken place in the context of other, non-school-based youth work and links with agencies, like the social services department and a unit called Pupil and Student Support based in the LEA. Young people 'at risk' are identified by the schools and then take part in a programme of activities based outside the school in converted premises on the local social services site. Community education staff note that it was necessary to develop open and trusting relationships with the schools before the projects could begin. Lines of communication had to be developed with management and staff, and issues like confidentiality had to be discussed and agreed upon before referrals were made by the schools.

A targeted activity programme
The referral and activity programme works like this:

- community education youth workers meet with school head and head of the chosen school year - Year 11 in the first instance;

- once school has identified pupils to participate, further meeting to discuss the needs of these individuals with school staff;

- schools complete referrals to the scheme, discuss this with young people and obtain consent from parents;

- youth workers meet young people individually to discuss what they want from the scheme;

- youth workers meet the whole group of young people;

- group runs for five weeks, following a 'syllabus' designed to encourage self-esteem and self-awareness, group and individual behaviour. Written work in common but participants are encouraged to work in their own style. Young people are encouraged to set their own rules and obey them while involved in the group. Each participant is held responsible for their own behaviour;

- in the sixth week teachers join the group to hear from the young people about the work they have been doing and their progress in it. Young people who do not wish to continue, or who are preventing other group members from progressing, are removed and replaced;

- group continues for a further five weeks, with trips and residential courses available to young people who meet certain criteria;

- out of school time, participants are helped to take part in other provision available in the locality.

These projects are considered to have improved school attendance and results, to have decreased the number of exclusions from school and to have helped young people move into training and jobs which were previously considered to be beyond their reach. They are interesting because they have been developed in liaison with school management and staff who have decided that youth work approaches will enhance the school's effectiveness. The projects are not seen as respite for the school, but as adding value to the school's work.

There are other examples of targeted interventions by the Youth Service in Cambridgeshire. For example, a school identified six young people in Year 11 as in danger of exclusion, and youth workers arranged a variety of residential adventure experiences for them, sometimes through voluntary sector specialist organisations like Fairbridge. In another school, the police and crime reduction staff from the local authority were also involved in a project for two targeted groups: Year 8 pupils who had formed a gang which was shop-lifting and encouraging other children to shop-lift; Year 7 pupils who were socially isolated, low in self-esteem and easily led. Youth club-type activities are offered to each group, and considerable success has been observed in the increase in self-esteem of both groups, and there has been a reduction in shop-lifting and vandalism locally.[54]

Targeted schemes occur in many areas, with slightly different characteristics in each.[55] An interesting variation in Surrey has created teams of staff from education welfare, educational psychology, teaching and youth work which provide activities to reinforce school links to the youth service, the probation service, the police, social services and voluntary organisations, or to create these links if necessary. The teams develop school-based activity projects that go on after school hours and work with parents and curriculum-based activities to encourage social responsibility, including community service. Schools provide a venue for the work of this team: a comfortable, central room in the school.

A specialist team to promote social responsibility

The scheme works with approximately fifteen young people in the school, who are identified through teachers, parents or other agencies, or who refer themselves. Pupils move in and out of the programme and some of its activities are open to other pupils. The support offered to help individual young people to cope is extremely varied. Examples include:

- individual timetables, facilitated by the youth worker or teacher, covering subjects identified within the national curriculum;

- alternative curriculum possibilities - a Caring for the Environment course at a local agricultural college, for example;

- special support in the classroom from the teacher in the team, for a targeted pupil or for the subject teacher;

- tuition for groups of excluded pupils in a youth club setting;

- pre-employment training for young people in their last year at school;

- a programme of extra-curricular activities facilitated by the youth worker in the team, based on the interest of the targeted young people but offered to the whole school;

- the establishment of self-help groups to look at issues like bullying and HIV and AIDS;

- residential opportunities to enable young people to meet with others and introduce them to resources in the community that are available to support them;

- specially designed courses on leadership and confidence-building.

The locality team is the core of this model and a new team is set up for each school in the programme. The inclusion of a teacher/co-ordinator, who spends 50 per cent of the working week on the programme, allows negotiation with other teachers on the best course of action for the young people who are targeted, and offers support to teachers in the classroom. The advice of the educational psychologist can help with the assessment and counselling of young people, the planning of individual behavioural support, and group work on social skills, stress management and self-esteem. Educational welfare provides a home-school link and contributes to support for young people who truant.[56]

Specialist youth leaders to support African-Caribbean young people

Another target, in the London Borough of Hammersmith and Fulham, are African-Caribbean young people. Here Home Office Section 11 funding has been used to appoint two specialist youth leaders, who work in a team with seven specialist teachers to provide support in the classroom, liaise with young people and their families, and set up individual personal development programmes inside and outside the schools. The latter involve a combination of leadership training, outdoor pursuits, first aid emergency training, life skills, basic education, confidence building and job training.

This team has established a strong relationship with schools and other education-based services. Regular meetings are held with year heads in schools, and many initiatives have emerged from collaboration with other agencies: careers guidance, social services, further education, leisure and recreation, community education, youth justice and the police. The approach has stemmed the flow of permanent exclusions of

African-Caribbean young people in the area, and has had some unlooked-for benefits. A youth work approach has meant that some young people have talked about personal problems that were previously unknown to the schools. There has been a growth of understanding in the schools about the out-of-school programmes in which young people participate, and involvement in these has been acknowledged in National Records of Achievement. Youth workers have facilitated the involvement of parents in home-school work programmes and more generally in school activities.

A model approach

Responses to disaffection and rising rates of exclusion may be locally designed and developed, like those described, may incorporate aspects of a national 'model' approach, or may use the latter in its entirety. For example, Cities in Schools is a nationally based voluntary organisation which offers "a three tier programme of services".[57] At the preventive level these involve training for staff who work with children and young people within and outside the school, covering subjects like behaviour management, the education of looked-after children, anti-bullying and welcoming parents. It also involves setting up projects of the sort noted elsewhere in this report: home-school links, after-school clubs, parental training and peer counselling. Reintegration work is designed "to return young people with multiple problems to mainstream primary and secondary schools through intensive, individual support packages that produce significant long-term savings".[58] The primary targets for this tier of the work are permanently excluded pupils aged from 8 to 14 years. Alternative intervention is aimed at young people whose education has broken down completely and takes place in further education and work experience settings.

Localities which use this model have local boards of management representing the local statutory, voluntary and business sectors. Cities in Schools reports that: "Nearly 150 business leaders and more than 200 representatives of schools, social services, LEAS, TECs, police and health agencies and local councillors sit on our boards of management."[59] Services working with young people in the locality are co-ordinated by this approach, which has also managed to involve over 1,000 employers, notably in the provision of work experience. In 1996, 75 projects were established in England and especially in Wales, in both rural and urban areas.

Summary

There are many examples of links between secondary schools and the agencies which use a *youth service* approach, starting from the individual young person and their needs.

- Collaborations between the youth service and schools are often *targeted* at young people who are *under-achieving* in school, *at risk of exclusion* or *at risk of offending*.

- Partnership projects may involve a range of professional resources, including the *police* and the *probation service* and staff specialising in *emotional and behavioural development*, based in education and social services departments.

- Although targeted projects are described as *preventive*, most are actually interventions in response to increasing levels of *exclusion* from schools. Many are quite *short-term* interventions.

- There are some examples of intervention projects *working with parents* as well as young people, but this is less likely to happen with older (over 14) pupils.

29

- Out-of-school programmes for young people who are having difficulties in school often incorporate *residential, adventure training* and *work experience* opportunities provided by the *voluntary sector* and *business.*

- Nationally based *voluntary organisations* offer *model programmes* which balance *personal development, work experience* and *community service* with *support for parenting* and *peer counselling.* Local management of such programmes draws on many community resources, private, voluntary and statutory.

- Most partnership programmes aim *to return or retain* young people in education and do not advocate changes in the school regime to address any institutional causes of disaffection.

6

Issues facing young people

The personal development, maturity, autonomy, creativity, confidence and self-esteem of young people are as important to society in general as they are to young people themselves.[60] The time available to attend to these directly in the National Curriculum is limited, but links with the community may offer opportunities to add value to the core subjects by making them a basis for meeting new people, going outside the school, undertaking self-directed work and so on. These are subjects where the judgement of 'effectiveness' will rest with young people and those who know them rather than relying on a testing system. There are no easily applied standard assessment tests for maturity.

The part of the school timetable which deals directly with the personal is called Personal and Social Education (PSE) which is not part of the National Curriculum. The weight given to it varies from school to school, though OFSTED reports appear to show that schools which give it a central role are more successful than those which do not. There is not much time for it in any school, however, and there is a great deal to cover.

What schools offer

The 1988 Education Act required schools to promote the spiritual, moral, cultural, mental and physical development of their pupils. The 1992 White Paper, *The Health of the Nation*, recognised the school as a setting for health promotion. Between 1986 and 1996 GEST funding supported the employment of drug and health education co-ordinators in most Local Education Authority areas, and some LEAs continue to fund these posts. Guidance on health education to run through the curriculum for 5- to 16-year-olds identified sex education (including teaching about HIV, AIDS and other sexually transmitted infections), mental health and substance use and misuse as essential. More recently, *Tackling Drugs Together* asked schools to develop policies on drug education and drug-related incidents and these are monitored during OFSTED inspections.

What young people need

Alcohol and drug misuse are significant risk factors for a range of health and social problems among young people. Between 1982 and 1991, the suicide rate among young men aged 15 to 24 rose by 75 per cent.[61] A Department of Health report on the mental health of young people estimates that 10-20 per cent of children and teenagers have worries or problems severe enough to need help in overcoming them. "In a typical health district, between 5,000 and 12,000 children could show psychiatric problems."[62]

Research studies in areas of Scotland and England indicate that young people have high victimisation rates for crimes like assaults and personal theft in public places, and that they also suffer high levels of harassment.[63] Yet they are often viewed as potential offenders rather than as vulnerable to crime. "Very often, too, vulnerable young people find it hard to discuss their difficulties with adults, and peers are overwhelmingly the group they turn to for support."[64] Bullying, both within schools and outside, has been highlighted as a basic reason for some of their worries and problems. On average, 25 per cent of primary pupils and 10 per cent of secondary pupils are bullied more than once or twice in any one term. Some pupils are bullied every day, often during their journey to and from school as well as in school.[65]

What may help

There are a range of issue-based organisations which offer information, support and help to young people about personal health, welfare and safety, either specifically or as part of a wider brief. Many of them produce materials for use in the classroom, offer training, conferences and events for teachers and may have regional or local networks of staff who offer support to schools. This work is likely to be preventive in the first place, but it can encourage the development of groups or activities which take place within and outside the school, and which involve young people actively in promoting good practice, supporting one another and solving problems.

Crime prevention groups

Local inter-agency groups may contract with national, issue-based organisations to develop activities within schools in an area. For example, crime reduction/prevention partnerships establish multi-agency groups to pursue work in schools. Membership of a local group is likely to include representatives from the social services, the probation service, the magistracy, the LEA, the youth and community service, a headteacher, the clerk to the magistrates, police schools liaison officers, community police officers, crime prevention officers, and sometimes a police HQ inter-agency department representative, victim support scheme, housing departments and so on. If there is one, the whole group will be co-ordinated by crime reduction staff from the local authority. Having examined the local situation, such groups may seek help from a specialist non-government agency like Crime Concern, which offers various approaches to youth crime prevention, including school-based programmes. The national agency helps the local partnership to establish these, liaising with the inter-agency group and providing it with materials, ideas and support for their direct work in the school.

Example of a local crime prevention partnership

A community policeman in Dorset, who regularly visits two secondary schools on his 'patch' and had previously given a talk on bicycle safety and organised a presentation from two specialist officers from the Police Drugs Prevention Unit, took the lead in supporting a group of young people from every year in both schools, to form a crime prevention group. The young people took the lead in choosing activities and carrying them out, both within the school and outside it. The police officer acted as their liaison with school staff and other agencies. The headteacher supported the group and facilitated connections within the school for it. She saw its virtue as being seen to be separate from direct school activities by the young people who ran it.

There are approximately 1,200 crime prevention groups of this kind in UK schools. They aim to help young people themselves deal with crime and anti-social behaviour through project work, empower them to identify their own worries about safety and welfare and to create solutions and enable them to contribute to crime prevention and develop their social awareness.

They have between three and 30 members and are run by young people themselves, supported by an adult, often from the police, the youth service, or a specialist co-ordinator, appointed by the multi-agency group.[66] Activities are varied and may be confined within the school, but some groups work with local shopkeepers to discover the extent of shop-lifting by young people and to help combat it by videos and dramas (demonstrating the consequences of being caught). Some campaigning work has been undertaken as a result of surveys of pupils about their fears - improvements in street lighting have been achieved, for example.

In a suburban area outside London pupils at a school group were consulted by a local train operator which had received complaints about vandalism and dangerous behaviour on its trains, and were helping to develop ways to counter this. In another school a police officer has co-ordinated a whole week of drugs awareness workshops, including a drama presentation by pupils and a visit to the school by users of a specialist drugs and alcohol agency. "The sincerity and honesty with which they answered the students' questions was stunning," reports one of the pupils.[67]

Personal safety and mediation

School crime prevention groups often address bullying, usually beginning with a school survey, working with school management on anti-bullying policies, and setting up support for young people. A lunch-time drop-in, where pupils can talk in confidence about what is happening to them (or what they are doing), boxes, into which notes can be dropped reporting incidents experienced, seen, or perpetrated, and peer-led counselling are among the initiatives reported. Several national agencies introduce and support anti-bullying programmes in schools, with similar ingredients to those described.

Offering mediation in disputes is one of these ingredients. Support from specialist organisations for counselling and mediation is well established and there is considerable experience of how to do it and how effective it can be. The Education for Mutual Understanding (EMU) Promoting School Project in Northern Ireland has established peer mediation in 13 primary schools and influenced schools in other parts of the UK through its contribution to teacher training and demonstrations of peer mediation techniques by children.[68]

Work with schools in England is carried out by community 'conflict resolution' projects in north and south London, Surrey, Bristol and the West Midlands, which run courses and workshops for staff, governors, parents, teachers and young people, funded by charitable trusts and foundations. These address conflict in the classroom, in the playground and at home, and aim to give students the skills to manage it. In one area community arts and theatre workshops are used by an agency which targets young people in youth work settings but works in schools at times.[69] There are some underlying links between these conflict resolution projects, but they are essentially local developments and vary in what they offer and how they do it.

Community arts projects

Community arts, theatre in education and peer mediation are used to raise other personal matters with pupils:

- A Theatre in Education drama production was the central thrust of a community-linked smoking initiative: "My dad thought it was excellent and my mum said she must stop smoking" (Year 5 pupil).

- A drama therapist will be working with selected groups of Year 9 students to explore the issue of aggressive behaviour.

- Misconceptions were broken down and friendships forged between students from two schools involved in a peer education project run by Coventry's Alcohol Advisory Service.

- A group of sixth-form girls from one of the city's comprehensives undertook six weeks of training so that they were able to deliver alcohol education to Year 9 pupils at a school for children with moderate learning difficulties.

- The tragic death of a local boy while playing 'chicken' prompted the Road Safety Unit to organise and fund a drama production called, 'Why did the chicken cross the road'.[70]

Preventive health projects

The above examples are provided by 'Health Promoting Schools'. The European Network of Health Promoting Schools (ENHPS) is a three-year development project supported by the World Health Organisation (WHO), the Commission of the European Communities and the Council of Europe. Thirty-eight countries are participating, each with a network of 'pilot' schools which develop health promotion and education through curriculum work and projects in the school and the community.

The UK membership of this project is conducted separately in England, Wales, Scotland and Northern Ireland. In England there are 16 pilot schools: six primary, seven secondary and three special schools which are matched with 32 'reference' schools which provide comparative data and controls against which the progress of the developments will be measured. Each school decides on its own activities within a framework of criteria which has three headings: the ethos and environment of the school, the curriculum, and family and community. The school liaises with other schools, parents/guardians and the community about its initiatives, and uses outside agencies and specialist services to advise, support and contribute to them. Schools in this scheme share experience and practices, and may also communicate with schools in other participating countries.

The Health Education Authority reports that LEAs, Health Authorities and schools which are not involved in the programme are interested in it, and that this may be affecting the situation reported in 1993: "There is a risk that health education may become increasingly marginalised in many schools, mainly because of the demands associated with the implementation of the National Curriculum, but also because of a shortage of suitably trained staff."[71] Among the issues identified by schools in the 1993 survey as needing development were: a reconsideration of the appropriate ages at which sex education, education about drugs, alcohol and tobacco should start; more effective sex education; and a need for greater emphasis on psychological health - coping with stress, coping with separation and bereavement, child protection, bullying and building self-esteem.

A specialist centre for HIV and sexual health in Sheffield provides a programme of training for teachers and offers resources and individual consultancy to schools. Twenty-five schools in the area use sexual health noticeboards provided by this agency, which give information about safer sex and the sexual health services available. The agency updates these regularly. Teams of staff have worked directly with pupils in some schools, but it is more common for primary and secondary teachers and school nurses to take part in sex education skills training courses. Resources made available to schools include Family Planning Association contraception kits. Training for teachers on issues facing young gay men and lesbians at school, and for parents to become peer sex educators is planned.

Health staff based in schools

It is difficult to establish how many school nurses are currently working in the UK. Professional associations estimate that there are between 3,000 and 4,000 and believe the number is falling. The usual pattern is for one nurse to cover several primary and secondary schools in an area, taking over from the health visitor when children start school. Practice varies but typically the nurse will run clinics where hearing and vision are tested, and will then screen children at intervals through their primary career and refer children for help if parents or teachers have a concern.

School nurses contribute to PSE classes in some schools. "I work closely with teachers. They may ask me to talk on a subject they're concerned about that's been highlighted nationally - glue-sniffing, say. I attend tutor's meetings at one secondary school where pastoral care and the issues that young people need to cope with are discussed. Staff there use me a lot and I go in on

Wednesday lunchtimes and have a room where anybody, staff or pupil, can come and see me."[72] This nurse is a trained counsellor and works as a volunteer with a young people's advisory service in her spare time.

School nurses note the *Health of the Nation* goal to reduce the teenage pregnancy rate by 50 per cent by the year 2000. Although the 1993 Education Act requires schools to provide sex education, it also gives parents the right to withdraw children from sex education classes. Some teachers are uncertain about giving contraceptive advice to girls under 16, and unwilling to allow them out of school in emergencies to visit family planning clinics. As a result it is difficult for young people to gain access to emergency contraception, and they may have worries about confidentiality if they tell a teacher that they have been sexually active.

Emergency health advice

A school nurse in Bath holds a drop-in clinic in a girls' school at 8.30 am on Mondays "in the medical room, right away from the main part of the school and when staff are having a headteacher's briefing. I thought this was an appropriate time to be available just in case unprotected sex had happened over the weekend."[73] This nurse had to persuade a local fund-holding General Practice to see young people who needed emergency contraception, even when they were not registered with the practice and were under 16 years of age. She did this by describing the scale of the need to a practice meeting: 40 young people had approached her for help in one year, there had been 10 pregnancies, seven aborted and three that had gone to term. The practice agreed, provided the nurse made the appointments and gave follow-up contraceptive advice. The GP surgery is near to the school, and girls can visit at break or in the lunch hour.

35

Sex education for young men

Several commentators note that sex education for young men is inadequate and that work is needed to combat traditional male stereotypes. Boys and young men may appear macho but are often hiding frightened, confused and vulnerable feelings. Small groups for boys, in which they are actively involved and which they help to develop, are recommended, with the involvement of community nurses who have family planning training.[74]

Peer-led sex education

Peer-led approaches to sex education as well as other health and personal safety matters are supported by a national collaboration between a charitable trust and a national voluntary agency, Community Service Volunteers (CSV): "Older students deliver a well-established programme of lessons in sexual health to younger students. They then train their pupils to present the same information to yet younger students, creating a cascade of informed and supportive student tutors throughout the school".[75] Students from London and Birmingham have worked in over 20 pilot schools and expansion is planned in three other parts of England.

The advice of experienced volunteers

A number of local projects to raise awareness of drug use and misuse have produced interesting partnerships between agencies and may include parents as well as young people. In the Isle of Wight prison officers and prisoners visit schools to work with small groups of sixth-formers. Prisoners respond to their questions about drug use. "The success of the sessions owed much to the honest responses of the prisoners to some penetrating questions they had not had to face in any other ways before." The prisoners' greatest asset is their credibility.[76]

Evaluations of health education with young people, particularly that which aims to prevent misuse of alcohol, suggests that peer education is more likely to be effective when peers have had personal experience of tackling the problem. Otherwise some doubts have been raised about the effectiveness of peer education as a preventive measure. It does, however, offer young people a role as educators, and an opportunity to increase their confidence, community involvement and self-esteem.[77]

Multi-agency support for disabled young people

Education for disabled young people in mainstream schools means that issues beyond the academic must be addressed. Particularly important are the nature of the young person's disability and any changes that may occur in it, mobility, support for physical development and social and self-help skills, and the affect of the disability on the young person's learning. The transition from primary to secondary school can pose new issues for disabled young people, and schools have to consider how, for example, the greater distances that have to be covered will be managed.

Assessing the needs of disabled children in a mainstream school

The SENCO at a secondary school in Dorchester described how a multi-agency group worked together for eighteen months before the admission of two disabled children to the school. Membership of the group varied but included the school doctor, a physiotherapist, the Educational Welfare Officer, and educational psychologist, occupational therapist, SENCOs from primary and middle schools, governors and headteachers.

The school is an upper school for 13- to 18-year-olds, with several buildings which are not linked to one another. Newer blocks with public access are also accessible for disabled people. There was pressure from the parents of two pupils with cerebral palsy that both should be transferred to secondary school with their peers. The children were already integrated into mainstream education and had established friendships. If they did not transfer to the school, they would have long journeys to a special school, which would be fatiguing for them. The SENCO notes that there was a negative climate in the school which needed to be changed: "Aiming to achieve something tangible - the modification of the school buildings - meant that the multi-agency team members were able to channel strengths, expertise and energy into achieving inclusion. We felt that once the children arrived, a more positive attitude would develop with the support of the multi-agency group".

This proved to be the case. The group applied to the DfEE for a grant to carry out building modifications which had been identified in consultation with the two young people and their families. Eighty-five per cent of the capital funding required was granted and the rest came from the school's budget. In this case change in the school was led by young people and their parents with the help of agencies from outside the school.

demands of the National Curriculum. Projects which address those issues which concern young people may be:

- *preventive*, in which case they are likely to be delivered within the school, sometimes with a contribution from teachers and also with peer-led support;

- *emergency intervention*, in which case issues of **confidentiality** are important to young people and may mean that school staff cannot be involved;

- about **bullying, sexual behaviour, drugs, health, alcohol** and **crime**;

- highly practical, showing useful **ways to avoid or deal with problems**;

- supported by staff from **all types of voluntary and statutory social care agency**.

Summary

It is interesting that here, as with the relationships between other organisations using a 'young person centred approach', there is some indication of tension between the school and partner agencies. Previously this has arisen in descriptions of projects carried out by youth workers. But it is apparent also in the description of support offered to young women by a school nurse, and in the comments from the Health Education Authority about the

7

'Wrap-around'

The need for children to have safe places to go for stimulation and care, after school and before it, during holidays and sometimes at weekends too, has quickly become recognised as a subject in which schools have an interest, and where they may act as providers. The national agency which promotes this approach, Kids Club Network (KCN), has a membership of 3,300 clubs in England and Wales. A recent survey of 1,900 showed that 45 per cent take place on school premises. The remainder use family centres, community centres, church halls or their own premises. Data on clubs collected from this survey suggests that approximately 1,000 are in rural areas.

Out-of-school care

Most after-school clubs are voluntary organisations managed by committees of parents, and representatives of the community, including school heads and teachers.

They received a boost when government funding for the development of clubs was channelled through local TECs in 1993. Grants vary in size, from £1,000 to £10,000, with an average size of £4,000. Support has also been available from a range of central statutory sources: the Department of Health, which makes small grants of up to £1,000 available to new and expanding clubs; the Home Office 'Safer Cities Programme', which has funded clubs in targeted areas, acknowledging their role in reducing juvenile crime; City Challenge, the Department of the Environment initiative for regenerating urban areas; childcare, including clubs, has featured in plans for

funding devised by local authorities; Inner City Task Force funds, and the Single Regeneration Budget (SRB) can also support club development as part of wider regeneration plans, as can the Rural Challenge initiative. The Rural Development Commission funds individual clubs in its priority areas and there are even circumstances where schools may be eligible for financial support from the European Social Fund. This is available for vocational training and employment schemes. There has been a close link between the provision of after-school care for children and the provision of training and employment for families. Local employers may support clubs, sometimes purchasing or subsidising places for the children of employees.

Clubs are also financed by fees paid by parents: typically between £10 and £20 per week, depending on the area, and between £25 and £30 per week in the holidays. Families receiving Family Credit and other benefits are able to offset childcare costs of up to £40 a week against their income and still receive the benefit. Social services may subsidise out-of-school care for individual children identified as 'in need' in order to provide support for them and their families. The provision of a nutritional meal before school is a feature of many clubs which open early.

Community involvement

"The initial idea behind starting an out-of-school club ... was to use under-used areas of the school for the benefit of the school community. I was interested in the idea as a parent governor and because, as a working family, my wife and I had experienced difficulties with our childcare arrangements and knew of other parents with similar problems."[78] In this case parents have worked in partnership with the school, local businesses and KCN to run a club as a voluntary organisation using the school premises. In some areas schools have used their own resources to contribute to such clubs, but KCN report that local management of schools can be a hindrance to new clubs: the rent demanded by governing bodies may raise the cost per child to levels that are prohibitive for poor families. In 1989 a circular to schools from the then Department of Education and Science (DES) noted that "Any use of school premises for childcare facilities must be made on at least a full cost recovery basis."[79]

On the whole, though, these developments have offered a new kind of partnership with parents and the local community, especially with the business community and the leisure and recreation departments of district councils, which have a responsibility for the provision of play. Community development staff in these departments have advised on the setting-up of clubs, which are sometimes constituted as community businesses. Their management has enabled parents to acquire skills as planners, developers and employers. They have also led to collaborations between schools in some areas.

Study Support

What goes on in a club is distinguished from what goes on in the school. An age-appropriate programme of activities and child-centred play is recommended by KCN, with a quiet area available for home-work and study. A different approach has come with the advent of Study Support, aimed, though not exclusively, at young people of secondary age, "to raise

achievement by motivating young people to become more effective learners through activities which enrich the curriculum and improve core skills. These activities take place on a voluntary basis out of school hours."[80] An evaluation conducted for the Prince's Trust notes various ways in which this is being provided, but these generally involve a centre, either at the school or in a community facility. A centre is staffed by teachers working after hours, youth and community workers, by student tutors, volunteers, and mentors from the local business community, and offers opportunities for coaching, advice, help and collaborative projects to young people who use it.

Over 500 schools have been helped to open Study Support Centres and the Prince's Trust intends to have a national network of 1,000 centres in operation by the year 2000.

Commentary on the experience so far emphasises the personal development opportunities given to young people from disadvantaged areas. The support is for self-study, for the development of independent learning habits and for personal and social development. This approach began in Strathclyde in 1990, with investment by the LEA so that schools could offer space for young people to do homework. An evaluation of this project was encouraging and led to the production of a Resources Pack by the Prince's Trust which was purchased for every school in Scotland by the Scottish Office. The concept has extended through the UK, with a set of criteria for good practice which include, for young people participating, a growth in self-esteem and self-assessment as well as achievement in school subjects and examinations.

Study Support is growing rapidly on two fronts: the Prince's Trust-Action operates an Awards Scheme, providing £1,000 to help good practice; 185 centres received such awards in 1996. The Trust has also encouraged the involvement of the business community in centres, nationally and locally. This may mean money, help-in-kind or volunteers. For example, in the West Midlands an Education Business Partnership (EBP), co-ordinated by a TEC, has linked with four schools and a local business to set up a Study Support Centre based on information technology for 35 young people. The skills have been identified as necessary by local employers, and as motivating and interesting young people by the schools. In other areas the catalyst for schemes has been the youth and community service: in Yorkshire, clubs in schools and community centres draw on a pool of volunteer tutors from the local university. A report notes that the community-based model "is more about life choices and about the place and purpose of educational achievement within that context ... it sets schooling in a wider social and economic framework."[81]

Growth is also likely to be affected by a longitudinal study of the value added to individuals and schools by Study Support Centres, which will examine what works and what are the key components of successful initiatives. Information will be collected on all Year 9 pupils from 50 schools, whether or not they attend Study Support Centres. Information on attainment and attendance will be supplemented by evidence about the pupils' attitudes to school, homework and self study. Teachers' expectations, attitudes and predictions for pupils will be incorporated in the data.[82]

Supplementary schools

There are a considerable number of study-support initiatives which have been developed by particular communities as a response to needs they perceive in their children.

Supplementary schools have a long history and are often started by refugee community groups as an effort to help children cope with an unfamiliar curriculum and unfamiliar language, or by minority ethnic groups concerned about the under-achievement of their children in mainstream schools. Mother-tongue schools derive from the need to maintain language, culture and identity. Both types of school claim to make an impact on the educational achievement of individual children. In London these schools once received a standard £1,500 from the Inner London Education Authority, but in recent years their main source of support has been the Trust for London, which has recently established a resource unit to help them with training, visits and materials. The Trust estimates that there are at least 400 schools of this sort in London alone, and more in other parts of the UK.[83]

The Resource Unit for Supplementary and Mother Tongue Schools reports that the size of these ventures varies from 15 to as many as 400 pupils, often meeting at weekends and attracting members of the particular community from a distance. Schools become a gathering point, offering social contact for families: "When you ask why they have come, people say, 'Because the children are the future'. There is a phenomenal commitment to these schools from the communities."[84] There are some links between supplementary schools and mainstream schools in Hackney, Tower Hamlets, Southwark and Islington where there are teachers who teach in both. Parents with little or no English can use the supplementary school as a way to communicate with the mainstream school, but experience of more extended links between the two is rare. This is an area which merits further research.

A borough-wide out-of-school initiative is set up as a summer university in Tower Hamlets. Twelve secondary schools, a further education college and a university college combine with the youth service to offer study and vocational courses, social education, arts and sports at the schools, specialist science and computer work at the colleges, arts and disability organisations and other bodies. Health, drugs and vocational training agencies provide on-site advice and run workshops. More than 2,200 young people participated in the first programme in 1996, and subsequently a marketing team of 58 young people were trained to 'sell' the programme to other young people and to become stewards and support workers for it during the summer. Other local authorities have expressed an interest in this approach.[85]

A recent report for the DfEE recognised three elements of extra-curricular provision: homework; 'curriculum extension' (of the sort provided in the Study Centres described above); and the traditional extra-curricular activities like sport, music and other interests which may be pursued after school or during breaks in the school day. The study showed that there was a correlation between the quality of schools as reflected in OFSTED inspections and the level of extra-curricular activity.[86]

The range of this activity and the potential for links with parents and the community is vast. Education Extra, a national network of schools, governors, parents, LEAs, TECs and others involved in out-of-school activities, records many of them in its newsletter: primary schools in a Single Regeneration Area will participate in a sports festival at a well-equipped local secondary school, where coaches from the city's professional teams will give them expert coaching in football, rugby, athletics, basketball; a secondary school notes that its own facilities are used by a local community boys' soccer club and the Ladies Netball League, and that the sports hall is in use every evening by local groups; another reports a school/community sports centre initiative where the school has linked with county and district councils, a local tertiary college, primary schools and a host of local sports clubs and sports governing bodies, and which was awaiting the result of a bid for funding to the Lottery Sports Fund.[87]

A comprehensive plan for school and community sports
The Sports Council for Northern Ireland has a highly developed programme for youth sport which aims to increase participation by young people in every kind of sport, raise standards of performance, increase the numbers of coaches and extend community use of school sports facilities. Schools are the focus for the programme, and its support staff include school sports co-ordinators in secondary schools who manage programmes of after-school activity linked to primary schools. The vision was to create introductory opportunities at neighbourhood level through primary schools, linking these to local opportunities in schools and sports clubs, and developing the opportunities at district level through the programmes of clubs, schools, leisure services and the youth service.

At Edmund Rice College, in Glengormley, which has been involved in the youth sport initiative since 1995, the school profile in the community and among primary schools has risen, and income has been generated through the letting of sports facilities to clubs.[88]

41

There is similar variety and enthusiasm in reports of school links with arts organisations. A teacher in South Shields reports close relations between his school and the local theatre, the Customs House, resulting in drama, dance, visual arts and other activities in the school, and a theatre exchange with a school in Germany. The theatre is also central to the Youth Arts week in the town, in which youth organisations and schools participate. Such relationships are more likely to develop where the theatre or arts organisation has a budget to work in education.

Summary

Although in many areas school heads have been active in helping to establish after-school care, this has been a movement based on parents and local community organisers, and the aim has been to promote the well-being of the child and family, rather than to improve educational achievement. School-based clubs try to make a clear distinction between their activities and those of the school, in order to offer children respite in a long day.

- In areas with high poverty indicators, *the provision of clubs and breakfast* before school opens has been seen as important in enabling children to participate fully during the school day.

- After-school care has emerged from partnerships between schools, *parents*, *community* and *neighbourhood* organisations in many areas.

- Some *private sector companies* have supported out-of-school care to help their employees.

- Study support differs from care in that it aims to *improve learning achievements* and employs *staff and volunteers* who coach and advise young people and help their *social and personal development.* Schemes are supported by *private sector companies* and the *youth service.*

- Supplementary and mother-tongue schools are typically set up and run by *volunteers from minority ethnic groups*. There are a few links with mainstream schools through teachers, but on the whole these are tenuous.

- Extra-curricular activities mean links with many interests in the community, especially those involving *sports and arts activities*. There is two-way traffic here, with school premises used by community-based sports and arts organisations, and some volunteer input into lessons and extra-curricular activities, and pupils participating in events held outside the school.

- The quality of school performance has been linked to *extra-curricular activity.*

8
School/business links

A survey carried out for the Department for Education in 1994-95 showed that 92 per cent of secondary schools and 58 per cent of primary schools had links with business.[89] There is no reason to suppose that these percentages have decreased. A number of mechanisms to support such links has been growing since the late seventies, when high levels of youth unemployment drew schools and business together under the auspices of the Manpower Services Commission (MSC) to improve the preparation of young people for work.

At that time there was concern among employers about poor skills among young school leavers and their lack of understanding about 'the world of work'. The improvement of education standards was seen as a way of securing greater labour market flexibility. That this remains a concern for the national business community is shown by a Confederation of British Industry (CBI) survey in October 1997, in which over 40 per cent of businesses considered that basic numeracy and communication skills among school-leavers were poor.[90] Explaining the tax benefits available to businesses which help schools, a government leaflet published in 1992 notes: "Both schools and businesses stand to benefit where employers involve themselves in the work of schools. The result is not only better-qualified school leavers for companies to recruit: direct assistance to schools also demonstrates a firm's commitment to its locality and can help it to present a positive image to the community."[91]

Links with a business may occur:

- **through direct contact**, generated by the school or the business: for example, Year 1 and 2 pupils from a primary school were taken on a visit to a local pig farm, the farmer has been to the school to talk to groups of children, further visits are planned; the managing director of a local business is invited to become a governor of a primary school; a business offers to sponsor a prize for achievement in the school;

- **collectively, as part of a local Education-Business Partnership or Compact** (EBP). This means that the efforts of local businesses are co-ordinated for increased impact, often by employees from the private sector on secondment, based at TECs, LEAs or both. For example, pupils in a secondary school were offered a day's programme of interview skills training and careers advice by staff from seven local companies, a local further education college and careers guidance; in another area a week of visits to industrial companies was arranged by the EBP for pupils from 500 schools in a borough; a course for teachers from twelve primary schools in a partnership area was hosted by one local company, to introduce a pack of materials developed by another EBP which links curriculum work in Science and Technology with the industrial processes to which they are related;

- *indirectly through local and national education/industry link agencies*: there are at least 30 of these, producing information, training materials, running courses and conferences and sometimes with their own networks of regional and local co-ordination. For example, "Working in partnership with Business in the Community, the international accountancy and management consultants KPMG have launched a major support programme to help the professional development of head teachers in inner city state schools." In this case senior staff from the company work as individual mentors with headteachers, providing them with advice and support on matters like "strategy development, action planning and performance measurement; financial budgeting and expenditure; leadership; human resource management including recruitment and professional development; institutional and cultural change; marketing and public relations."[92] In return, the private sector mentors are expected to benefit from the insights they gain into public sector organisations subject to public accountability, financial restraint and under pressure to improve performance.

Why business gets involved with schools

Motivation for involvement on the part of the businesses, as well as the sort of activities undertaken, varies according to the type of school. A business may work with local primary schools because many of its own employees have children there; they are a very visible part of most communities; it is possible to influence the attitudes of young children towards matters like wealth creation, science and technology and careers for women in industry. A relationship with secondary schools may be chosen because the company wants young people to see its work as a potential career; there are opportunities to

contribute to the secondary curriculum, which is beginning to reflect the needs of the workplace; pupils are potential future customers; pupils on work experience placements can be helpful to the company; partnership with schools can offer management development opportunities for company staff (see the KPMG example quoted above); schools as centres of learning can provide support to small, local businesses. Where businesses work with special schools, additional reasons are cited: to provide support for disadvantaged members of the community and to demonstrate corporate goodwill and commitment to equality of opportunity.[93]

Typical links between companies and primary schools

- Visits to the company's premises by schoolchildren.
- Visits to the school by company staff to talk about their work or special subjects.
- Provision of materials for classroom work.
- Staff volunteers (to listen to reading, help with sport).
- Sponsorship of materials.
- Curriculum projects.
- Secondment of teachers to the company.
- Membership of the governing body.

Typical links between companies and secondary schools

All of the above plus:
- Industry days and careers events.
- Enterprise activity and work simulation.
- Work experience and work shadowing.
- Tutoring and mentoring.

For mutual benefit

These links, then, are a two-way process, the principal aim being to improve the achievement of schools for the eventual benefit of business. Schools and businesses are encouraged by umbrella bodies to justify the place of these relationships in the National Curriculum through the contributions made to pupils' learning in core and foundation subjects. A programme which aims to root such contributions in a 'whole school' approach, balancing the academic curriculum with the personal development of pupils, is called 'Pathways Toward Adult Life' (Pathways), and was originally piloted by a consortium of 16 of the largest companies in the UK and the Corporation of London, through the London Enterprise Agency. The 17 schools involved linked classroom learning to 'the world of work', and used work as a context for young people to acquire key skills like communication, problem-solving and team-work. It is described by the Minister for Education as giving schools a means "of managing those many vital areas of personal development that at present have little formal structure."[94] By teachers, however, it is seen largely as a way to assist young people in the transition from school to work. "Pathways has given our children the opportunity to experience different perspectives on the world of work. It has provided the opportunity to make contacts with the business community thus enabling them to work alongside us in a clearly focused way. It has given an insight into possibilities for the future."[95]

In contrast to the 'whole school, whole curriculum' approach, some schools have found that giving a select group of young people access to a real-work environment as a privilege can create motivation in them which is otherwise lacking. In one school it has been offered to 20 boys from Year 9, who are given an opportunity to work with people outside the school for two days a month for one year. The aim is to give the boys an insight into the demands of the workplace and into how they will be dealt with in it. They are required to

organise themselves and their work schedule, prepare for the tasks, work hard and report back on their experiences in the classroom.[96] The majority of the businesses participating in this scheme are small enterprises.

Summary
This has been a growth area since the increase in youth unemployment in the late seventies led education and employers to liaise more closely about the content of the curriculum. This liaison was directed at the production of the kind of school-leavers who would 'fit' the needs of business, and it is seen, too, in the influence that employers have had on the courses offered by universities.

- Businesses support local schools as part of *corporate responsibility*, or *community involvement* policies.

- Links involve children and young people *visiting companies*, or company staff *visiting schools*, for one-off presentations or to work as *volunteers.*

- The private sector also offers schools advice and training in *school management* and staff may serve in *school governing bodies*.

- Most partnerships between schools and business have the *preparation of young people for work* as their main objective.

- Projects which 'place' young people in work situations with local businesses as an alternative to classroom study have been found to *improve motivation*, especially of young men.

- Relationships with business have influenced *what is taught* in the classroom, as well as how schools are run.

9 Community involvement and citizenship

The Schools Curriculum and Assessment Authority has defined four 'shared values' on which schools are encouraged to base mission statements, development plans and relationships within and outside the school: valuing ourselves, valuing others, valuing society and valuing the environment.[97] These imply education by experience, learning situations beyond the classroom, and contact beyond the school.

Peer-led initiatives present one means of pursuing these values. Encouraging young people to work outside the school in collaborative ventures to help people in need, contribute to community events and improve the environment, present others. The community is seen as offering learning experiences which will help young people to become 'good citizens', but will also (and this is emphasised) help them to develop core skills, like working as part of a team, solving problems, managing their own time and presenting themselves, which are valued by employers.

Community service

In the past this kind of school-based project was known as 'community service' and tended to take place outside the curriculum. It received attention when schools were looking for activities to interest unwilling pupils: after the raising of the school leaving age, for example. It was also seen as a way of preparing young people for the world of work. Its reputation with schools suffered when it became a means of punishing offenders through community service orders, and when it was combined with training for young unemployed people. The development of care in the community made it more difficult for schools to organise activities. People in need in the community were more widely dispersed. Institutions like hospitals were less likely to have a volunteer organiser who could 'place' young people in useful tasks.

National support for school 'service-learning' projects

Despite these changes, there is still a good deal of recognisable 'community service' being carried out by schools. A national project, sponsored by a bank at a cost of £5 million for five years, offers awards of £3,000 to individual schools and £7,000 to groups of schools "allowing them to tackle issues that matter to them and their local community."[98] Three hundred and eighty-one schools have received grants for two-year projects under three headings: peer learning, community service and environment. The first is divided into three categories:

- peer tutoring, where pupils help others, usually younger, with reading. Secondary schools and college students work with children in primary schools;

- peer education, on topics like HIV and AIDS, drugs and alcohol and anti-racism;

- peer support, listening and counselling other young people about bullying, stress, bereavement or emotional problems.

These activities may go on within the pupil's own school or elsewhere. There are some indications (as there are with crime prevention projects) that the bulk of this work happens on the school premises.

Community service projects focus on need outside the school, particularly among elderly and disabled people, and children and young people with special needs. For example, sixth-form students are placed in hospitals and units which treat patients with severe disabilities; students from a secondary school accompany disabled children from a special school on outdoor pursuits; pupils provide a library outreach service to housebound and elderly people in a rural area. Again, there is some evidence that work with disadvantaged groups often happens on the school premises rather than in the community. Elderly people are invited to the school for Christmas entertainments or lunch; at one school they come for introductions to information technology given by pupils, at another a newspaper is prepared by pupils and distributed in the community. Such projects offer students opportunities to choose, plan and manage their own activities. The national programme cited above estimates that students are partly responsible for 70 per cent of the funded projects and have total responsibility for 27 per cent.

Multi-school community service run by young people
The most fully-fledged example of local community service is over thirty years old and has been thoroughly documented.[99] It operates through a network of over 20 schools, including special schools, and delivers an average of 2,000 hours of service each week in the community. The work is organised into four main focus areas - with children, young people, disabled people and elderly people - and each focus has an action group which meets monthly to plan and carry out activities. Action groups are comprised of representatives from the schools and they organise continual weekly activities which require regular commitment from young people: children's clubs, teas for elderly people, peer education groups; and initiate one-off events, like trips, holidays and festivals. Individual volunteers are placed in situations which suit their skills and where they can contribute most effectively, and there is traffic between the curriculum and the community programme, with classroom-based learning and placements in the community supporting one another.

This project has nine full-time members of staff and is supported by schoolteachers and adult volunteers from the community. It is funded by its own fundraising, the local authority through the social services department and youth service, the LEA, district councils, and sponsorship from local businesses. There is a multi-agency advisory committee on which young people are represented, and a management committee. Schools are fully involved in the management and support of this work, and the liaison system of school representatives enables governing bodies and year heads within the school to be up-to-date with the project. Widespread recognition of the quality of this work has not resulted in replication of the project elsewhere.

Environmental work

Involvement in environmental projects and sustainable development has offered schools in many areas an opportunity to work collaboratively with local planners. Agenda 21, agreed by 154 countries at the 1992 Earth Summit in Rio de Janeiro, is a programme for sustainable development at national and local

47

level. Staff in local planning departments are encouraged to plan with local people to develop responses to traffic, employment, health, recreation, conservation and preservation, rivers and other local issues.

The World Wide Fund for Nature (WWF-UK) reports a growing involvement of local authorities in this process, with school contributions through projects like nature conservation and wildlife areas in school grounds or nearby, and tree and shrub planting; establishing environment education centres in schools, for wider use by the community; partnerships between schools and local businesses to look, for example, at waste minimisation and energy efficiency; the preparation of consciousness-raising materials - videos, newsletters, dramas - by young people for wider dissemination. A scheme to encourage households to reduce waste and use energy efficiently is beginning to work in schools, combining curriculum approaches (the environment is a cross-curricular theme in the National Curriculum), and action by children within schools to audit and change practices which effect the environment, with a family pledge to implement similar audits and improvements in the home.[100]

> *Benefits of environmental projects for pupils*
> A national agency which supports regeneration and environmental work through over 40 local offices, reports that collaboration in local planning offers:
>
> • children the opportunity to collect information from the community using research methods, (interviews, surveys, videos etc.);

> • a chance for children to offer views about their own experience of the environment, in a context where they have equal weight (and where they may be very different from those of other groups in the community);
>
> • practical activities, often out-of-doors, "A group of autistic young people planted a willow tunnel, a living piece of play equipment ... creating an interesting and permanent feature";
>
> • participation in projects that have the potential to make a visible change - to derelict sites, for example.[101]

Direct involvement in planning

A planning technique in use by some authorities, both for Agenda 21 and to address the specific needs of parts of an area - in villages where previously reliable sources of employment have ended, for example, or where a piece of land is to be developed for community benefit - has been designed to engage children and young people, and to overcome limitations of language and experience which may make it more difficult to involve them. A scale model of the area is created by participants in the planning exercise, which is recognisable and depends upon their local understanding and knowledge. The model is supplemented by information collection to discover what changes local people want and to develop action plans to implement them. Apparatus like this, which is being updated in collaboration with an LEA to reinforce links across curriculum subjects as well as with geography, provide a forum for schools and children to meet with local community groups, and may cross-fertilise relationships between school and family.[102]

Promoting democratic dispositions

Activities designed to promote 'citizenship' among young people are inextricably entwined with the kind of practices already described in this section. In Northern Ireland two primary schools gained a Gulbenkian Award for citizenship for making and distributing window boxes in their respective deprived neighbourhoods; young people formed a drama group to perform work relevant to the problems of their neighbourhood, like drug abuse and joy-riding. The extra element implicit in citizenship is the opportunity to participate in and learn from experience about the democratic institutions and processes of the state.

There is evidence of activity throughout the UK, focused on the UN Convention on the Rights of the Child, led by local authorities and supported by non-government organisations, especially national voluntary bodies which work with children. It is tending, therefore, to be based outside schools, in youth service territory.[103] The Children's Consortium on Education, a grouping of these voluntary bodies, has produced a framework for the development of education for all children consistent with their rights under the convention. This notes that when the Committee on the Rights of the Child examined the UK record in implementing the Convention, in 1995, key recommendations were made about education practice. Among these were:

- teaching about children's rights should be incorporated in the curriculum of teacher education;
- consideration should be given to including the Convention in the school curriculum;
- more emphasis should be given to providing children with opportunities to express their views on the running of schools.

In comparison with practice elsewhere in the world, the education service in the UK has not taken a strong lead in informing children and young people about their rights under the Convention.[104]

Within schools the commonest mechanism for democracy and participation is the school council. In one LEA where school councils in both primary and secondary schools are being encouraged, sixth-form pupils were invited to a consultation with elected members at a council meeting, where they were able to make a case for improved leisure facilities for young people. This level of attention is unusual. A study of school councils finds that they are extremely fragile and difficult to sustain. "Typically, students find participation in school council affairs fairly frustrating and the most common complaints focus on the generally trivial levels of business handled by the councils. Interestingly, when heads wish to consult all pupils on matters such as behaviour policies, they often tend to bypass the council, going direct to tutor groups, further undermining the status of the council in the eyes of the whole school and of councillors themselves."[105]

Summary

Schools are encouraged to develop values in young people which require involvement with the community. Opportunities are offered for:

- *community service* - helping other people in the community - both inside and outside the school;

- *'service learning'* which links the community service experience either to the curriculum or to personal development; the idea is that these are not peripheral activities but central to the school's agenda;

- *peer learning* - which is divided into *peer tutoring*, where students help others, usually younger and usually with reading; *peer education* on subjects like HIV and AIDS and drugs; *peer support* for young people who have problems;

- *managing projects*, designing and running them with adult support but minimum intervention;

- *relationships* with a range of people from the community, including many whom young people might not otherwise meet;

- young people to *contribute, have a role* and *be recognised* and *thanked*;

- young people to draw on their own *personalities, interests* and *skills* in ways which may not be required in school;

- learning *at first hand* or by experience, in settings which may be *challenging,* from people who may need *patience* and *understanding*;

- *participating as equals* with other members of the community, in collaborative planning or *environmental projects*, for example.

- being *a role model* for younger people.

10

The community school

The National Curriculum is now established which means that much of the practice described so far has been developed as 'add on' to the school's curriculum activities. Because of the priority given to the curriculum, the additions vie with one another for curriculum time, and try to make a case for inclusion within it. Thus involvement in planning with local community groups is associated with geography by back-up materials, energy efficiency schemes are marketed as helping to satisfy the requirements of the National Curriculum across every subject, and so on.[106]

The idea of the community school derives from an altogether different strand of educational thinking. This sees the school as a learning facility both for adults and children; inclusive, rather than specialist, flexible and responsive to the needs of the community, rather than rigid and authoritarian. The thinking goes back a long way. In 1924, Henry Morris, Chief Education Officer for Cambridgeshire, in his memorandum on the village college, described a place which would be the centre of learning, culture and social life. Sometimes dismissed as only applicable in rural situations, the results of his philosophy and the village college model spread in a series of fits and starts across the UK. They were most visible in his own county and in Devon and Northumbria, but also in urban situations. They enjoyed a boost in Coventry and Leicestershire in the sixties, and there are many individual examples of purpose-built community schools and of schools which have been converted to the community approach. (This has often been led by heads who learned their lesson in the heartlands of

community education and took it with them when they assumed a headship elsewhere. The number who have done this are an advertisement for the approach.) There is no agreed figure on the number of schools of this type in the UK, though a number of between 800 and 1,000 is sometimes cited.[107]

Life-long education

The distinguishing characteristic of these schools is a commitment to education as a lifelong process in which everyone has a part to play. Adults learn in the school, often in the classroom alongside young people. In one urban example the ratio of adults to young people is 3:1. The school premises are open until late at night, with the 'plant' facilities - sports and drama facilities, meeting spaces and workshops, classrooms and, often, a bar - open at weekends. Youth work is incorporated into the community school, as are many of the 'add-ons' described already. Pre-school groups, parenting support, basic skills, inter-action with the community all occur in this context. Community schools have staff who are responsible for these processes and teachers who subscribe to them.

There is anecdotal evidence that 'failing schools' can be improved by conversion to the holistic approach, but that introducing it takes time. For example, a Manchester girls' school which had "lost the community's confidence" five years ago, and had falling rolls, began by offering a few 'taster' courses for adults in the summer term and appointing a community education co-ordinator. The following school year saw an increase of adult courses to two afternoons and one night a week, the school information technology equipment was made available for use by the community and informal parenting sessions were introduced. After five years these two strands have grown into adult education on three days and nights of the week (with crèche) and a fully fledged community association which runs events and advises the school governors on lettings policy. The school's reputation is high, with a full roll and waiting lists for places. In other words, the conversion has been a vehicle for whole school improvement.[108]

> *Expanding the premises for community use*
>
> In Hartlepool, where a school had been identified by OFSTED as causing concern, and numbers had fallen from 1,250 to 490 pupils, the change in philosophy was linked with applications for funding from the European Commission and the Department of the Environment. In order to develop adult education, more space and better facilities were needed. Reception and crèche areas, new classrooms, and floodlighting for outdoor sports fields were provided by the investment. Local teams using the sports facilities guarantee to give two hours of coaching to young people in return. The use of sports facilities adds an extra £100,000 per annum to the school's turnover.[109]

Community education and young people

Advocates of the community education approach note that it supports young people by:

- presenting the school as a convivial place to which people of all ages want to come;

- presenting learning as desirable for people of all ages, something to which adults wish to return, and in which pupils themselves will be able to continue to participate;

- giving opportunities for interaction with adults, informally and as part of a common enterprise;

- enabling parents to participate in the school to meet their own needs as well as in their parental role;

- offering a range of learning situations to suit individual young people;

- raising the reputation of the school and, by association, the young people, throughout the community, and especially with local employers.

The amalgam of personal development and curriculum-based learning is designed to be seamless in this setting, as is the relationship between young person, family, community and school. Relationships between community schools and local health and social services staff should become closer than they are when schools do not subscribe to this philosophy, but there is no evidence to confirm that this is actually the case.

Why not all schools?

The community education argument is an attractive one which begs the question: why are more schools not taking this approach? The first answer is a practical one: they are not built for it. If the community school can expect as much as a 75 per cent increase in the numbers of people using the 'plant', it needs space. Of the 18,000 locally managed community buildings identified in a recent survey, only around 200 appear to be based in schools.[110] This figure does not include purpose-built community schools, where management is in the hands of the governing body. Local management of budgets and collaborations with the private sector, together with the availability of regeneration funding in some areas, should offer some schools an opportunity to expand their 'plant' in a community direction.

Other factors which have inhibited 'conversion' include: timetable pressures, security fears and the attitudes of school staff. Non-teaching staff in particular are often quoted as central to the success of a community approach: it may depend upon the willingness of caretakers and ancillary staff to welcome the community into the school. Teacher training does not provide an adequate introduction to the community school, and it is significant that its strongest advocates are people who have learned about it through experience rather than through training.

Summary

Community education is a specific approach with a long tradition. It sees education as:

- a *life-long process* available for everyone;

- including *children* and *adults learning alongside* and *from one another*;

- taking place in the *evening* and at *weekends,* not just in school hours;

- involving *every kind of activity*, including *interest-based, entertainment* and *sports and arts* activities;

- generating *excitement* and *conviviality* in the community and giving the school a *central role* as a place where everyone will find *something to suit their needs.*

- involving the community in *designing and running* the whole programme.

Difficulties encountered in spreading this tradition have been:

- the *unwillingness* of education policy-makers to embrace the whole philosophy;

- the need for *suitable* school premises;

- the demands on *school managers* who need to understand and implement a *community development approach*;

- the demands on teachers, who have little *training support* for these approaches;

- the demands on *communities* who have to work hard if a community school is to work.

Nevertheless, the community education approach has been introduced successfully into schools which were formerly deemed to be failing.

11 | Conclusion

The school has always been sandwiched between delivering what society wants it to do and requiring the support of society in order to do it. The social contract here is difficult to balance. At a time when the school's part of the contract has been clarified in a National Curriculum - a set of standards and an apparently agreed agenda for the 'effective school' - along comes another set of demands, not part of that agenda but without which, it seems, it cannot be achieved.

The effectiveness of a school is a collective result, composed of the individual achievements of everybody involved in it. There are aspects of the life of children and young people outside the school which make individual achievement within the school more or less likely. Recognising these influences, working with them and supporting them, is accepted as a responsibility of schools and expressed in central government policies which encourage links between school, family and community. This seems eminently sensible.

There are nagging difficulties, however. The preoccupation of education with what goes on inside the school premises has shifted the balance somewhat away from the development and learning opportunities that individual children and young people may find elsewhere. We know that this happens. Any individual recalling how they learned will cite experiences that were nothing to do with school. Sometimes it seems that they were actually effective experiences precisely *because* they were nothing to do with school. The child or young person was exposed to learning opportunities which made demands on their individual interests, personality or skills and which emphasised their autonomy. Educationalists recognise the importance of individual personal development and the contribution that random, unorchestrated experience may make to it. But helping to provide these opportunities without incorporating them into a curriculum and basing them in the classroom is challenging. It can be argued that the more schools concentrate on curriculum-based learning the more difficult it will be for them to develop relationships with a wider community.

Many projects and activities have been generated to make links between schools and the 'outside world'. How can a school select the activities which will work best? Can schools bear the weight of expectation that is accumulating around them? Schools may be attractive as units of social organisation but they are, after all, only children, teachers, a building.

Pressures on the school

The most pressing shortages are of time, space, and energy. Resources are less of a problem. Many of these activities come with funding - indeed, this may be what makes them attractive - and they also have access to funding, from private, statutory and charitable sources. Time is the great problem. Many of the developments mentioned in this report have required some time from class teachers, and it is often the contribution of class teachers which is cited as the key ingredient for success.

Yet teachers find that the demands of the National Curriculum leave them with little time. They are supposed to spend 20 per cent of this on non-curricular activities, but in reality many find it difficult to fit much in. And there is a minimum of help provided by their training. It is difficult to facilitate contributions from outside the school, particularly when these need to be linked to curriculum goals. Volunteer organisers in the community know that volunteers need careful placement, management and support. Community workers know about supporting collective action by local people to help them achieve goals which they set themselves. Understanding how to do this is not a part of teacher training.

There are demands, too, on parents' time. Working hours and school hours coincide. It may be logistically impossible to participate in parenting support, especially for lone parents, or where both parents are in employment. It is difficult to get parents to evening meetings. Which home-school programmes are most successful in getting parents to participate? And how are parent volunteers in the classroom recruited and managed? They may provide extremely useful extra help, but they need preparation and support from the class teacher, who has limited time.

The solution may lie in offering a home within the school to expertise from outside it. The projects which are doing this are all rather new and untested, but they will provide interesting information about the impact of other agencies on the way schools work. The example of a multi-agency team assessing a school prior to the admission of disabled young people suggests that attitudes may change as a result.

The need for planning

The locally managed school is part of a market place. 'Packages' are being offered to it, in order to persuade it to add value to its core task - to deliver the National Curriculum. The packages have been developed by organisations which specialise in certain subjects: family support, health, drugs, youth 'at risk', environmental regeneration and so on. Much of what they offer is based on practice developed elsewhere, especially in the United States, and much of it is similar. It is surprising, for example, how frequently 'peer education' features as an element in these programmes.

How effective are they? Many come with evaluation reports based on the experience of schools and communities in the UK where they were first implemented. These have been carried out by people of integrity and experience. But there are no comparative studies and there is little evidence about long-term impact. Not surprising, since hardly any of the programmes have been operational for more than ten years and there has been little follow-up research.

Where systematic review of programmes and research has occurred, the results are often disappointing. In an unpublished review of health education with young people for the prevention of alcohol misuse the conclusion is that 'nothing much works'. Most local programmes have unclear goals and make little scientifically acceptable effort to assess outcomes. These criticisms could be levelled more widely - at the evaluation reports distributed as part of the marketing of 'packages' to schools, for example.

The marketing of these programmes is often elaborate. It has benefited from the skills of private sector sponsors. As well as training,

55

materials and staffing, schools may be offered funding to participate in these programmes, and there is often an award scheme, which draws attention both to school, programme and sponsor.

A possible drawback of national specialist programmes is that they fill a space in schools which could be filled by local agencies, developing local responses to the same issues. In fact, many national agencies do work through partnership with local services. But if a school is to develop relationships with local policemen and social workers, health visitors, and speech therapists, artists and footballers, there is really no substitute for direct contact and the laborious process of getting to know one another and discovering where mutual benefit may lie.

Some filter is required to enable schools to select what is most appropriate to add on to the core programme, and to judge what is likely to work best. The Local Education Authority is the obvious intermediary, and where the filter function has been assumed, a coherent programme of home-school development has resulted, with flexibility for individual schools within a general framework established by the authority, which provides extra staff support to carry it out. This makes sense, but it is not widespread. It is more likely to occur where the authority has a community education tradition.

A typology of school-family-community links

To understand the complex web of activities which attempts to bind school, family and community together, to encourage family involvement in the school and a more prominent role for the school in the lives of family and community, the following categories are useful.

- *Decision-making and management of the school*
  Parents and other community representatives participate in the governing board, parent-teacher associations and advisory committees.

- *Communication between home and school*
  Schools tell families about the child's progress, through letters, reports, phone calls and meetings.

- *School support for families*
  Any help which schools provide for families in discharging their responsibilities to children, such as health, guidance, supervision and creating home conditions that support school achievement and social behaviour.

- *Family and community help for schools*
  The involvement of parents, community and employee volunteers who assist teachers, managers and children in classrooms or in other aspects of the school's activities.

- *Encouragement of learning activities at home*
  Help which the school gives to families - either in response to their requests or because the school is anxious that the child's work should be reinforced - to develop learning in the home that can be co-ordinated with the child's learning at school.

- *Collaborations and exchanges with community agencies*
  The involvement of, or connections with, outside agencies that provide access to community and support services for children.

- *Community education*
  Learning opportunities managed by community associations for all age groups, but often operating in school holidays, or as supplementary schools

Development is slowest in the latter two categories, which are furthest from the school curriculum culture. Children's Services Plans are bringing agencies together at the strategic level, but collaboration is not always filtering down to the field social worker, health professional, or class teacher. When it does happen, it can be very practical and effective: the school nurse, whose clinic is described on page 35, is a good example of practical intervention. These links take time, and require a basic understanding of professional roles. Some teachers do not have this, nor is it a part of teacher training.

Further questions raised by this overview
A broad-brush exercise like this always raises many questions, some requiring further investigation.

- Schools consider themselves less 'stigmatised' than some social agencies, because they are offered to the whole community, not only those who have been identified as 'in need'. If they develop targeted work to support families where children are 'in need', will that become stigmatised in the same way that involvement with social workers has been? Or can social work involvement in the school help to 'rehabilitate' social workers by giving them a more general, advisory function? The project in Manchester described on page 18 will provide important evidence about the impact of using the school as a centre for services.

- Is the emphasis on educational achievement and its measurement affecting other crucial childhood experiences, like play, exploration, and risk-taking? Some commentators have raised this concern.

- Family and community support for children in middle childhood is less clearly focused than that for young children and young adults. What support do children in transition need? What is the right balance between family and individual support as the child grows?

- Does the pressure on teacher time mean that all schools should have special home-school liaison staff to co-ordinate and run activities?

- There are many preventive education programmes for young adults; less is available for young people who are in trouble. Even where youth workers or counsellors are attached to schools, the back-up services available for young people with drug or mental health problems are sparse. Is the school being expected to deal with problems because there is nobody else who can?

- What can schools learn from the 'empowering' practice of community development? Do supplementary schools help communities and individual children in the way they claim, and how can mainstream schools learn from them?

- Community educators suggest that the presence of adults learning in the school has an impact on the behaviour of young people. American research confirms this, but more investigation is needed in the UK.[111]

57

- What do work experience and community service opportunities contribute to the personal development of young people? There is plenty of anecdotal evidence, but can this be measured?

- Links between schools and business have been a growth area, both for training and work experience but also via the specialist packages offered to schools by agencies and sponsored by the private sector. There may be a gap between the way these links are seen by the private sector and the way they are perceived by schools. Are they as effective as the glowing reports, or is this another aspect of a marketing approach?

- If the community education approach provides a viable mechanism for school, family and community links, should it not be examined more closely, so that schools can understand exactly what they will need to convert to this approach, in terms of resources as well as philosophy?

- Are children and young people actually part of the community, or is their experience becoming more and more circumscribed: by the time they have available, by fears for their safety, by limitations on what they are allowed to do? Is a completely new approach to childhood, perhaps based on the UN Convention on the Rights of the Child, necessary? An interesting discussion on this matter has just begun.[112]

References

1. National Commission on Education (1993) *Learning to Succeed*. Routledge. London.

2. Smith, G. (1995) 'Urban education: current position and future possibilities' in *Access and Achievement in Urban Education: Nature of improvement*. OFSTED. London; Smith, G. and Noble, M. (1995) *Education Divides: Poverty and schooling in the 1990s*. CPAG. London.

3. Power, A. and Tunstall, R. (1995) *Swimming against the Tide: Polarisation or progress on twenty unpopular estates 1980-1995*. Joseph Rowntree Foundation. York.

4. OFSTED (1993) *Access and Achievement in Urban Education: A report from the office of Her Majesty's Chief Inspector of Schools*. HMSO. London.

5. Sammons, P., Hillman, J. and Mortimore, P. (1995) *Key Characteristics of Effective Schools*. OFSTED. London.

6. DfEE (1997) *School Governors: A guide to the law*. HMSO. London.

7. Department of Health (1995) *Protecting Children: Messages from research*. HMSO. London; Audit Commission (1994) *Seen but Not Heard: Co-ordinating community child health and social services for children*. HMSO. London; Utting, D. et al. (1993) *Crime and the Family: Improving child rearing and preventing delinquency*. Family Policy Studies Centre. London.

8. Tunstill, J. 'The concept of children in need: the answer or problem for family support?', *Children and Youth Services Review*. Vol. 17, pp. 651-664.

9. National Commission on Education (1996) *Success Against the Odds: Effective schools in disadvantaged areas*. Routledge. London.

10. DfEE (1997) *Excellence in Schools*. The Stationery Office. London. DfEE.

11. Sweinhart, L. J., Barnes, H. V., and Weikart, D. P. (1993) *The High/Scope Perry Preschool Curriculum Models through Age 27*. High/Scope Educational Foundation. Ypsilanti, Michigan.

12. Birmingham City Council (July 1997) *Leisure Link Newsletter* Issue 1.

13. OPCS (1994) *Parents' Views of Daycare*. HMSO. London.

14. See 9 above.

15. National Children's Bureau (1996) *Four Year Olds in School: What is appropriate provision?* Child Facts. London.

16. DfEE (1997) *Progress with Partnerships*. Early Years Network. London.

17. Ibid.

18. Smith, T. (1987) 'Family centres: prevention, partnership or community alternative?' in MacFarlane, J. A. (ed.) *Progress in Child Health* Vol. 3. Churchill Livingstone. Edinburgh.

19. Perry, C. (1997) 'How to put children first and reduce crime' in *Family Support Network Newsletter*. UEA. Norwich.

20. Cameron, R. J. (1997) 'Early intervention for young children with developmental delay: the Portage approach' in McConachie, H. (ed.) *Child: Care, Health and Development* Vol. 23. Blackwell. Oxford.

21. SCEC (1995) *Community Education and Schools: A report on collaboration between Scotland's primary and secondary schools and community education services*. SCEC. Edinburgh.

22. Klimes, I. et al. (1996) *The Family Connections* (unpublished).

23. Smith, C. (1996) *Developing Parenting Programmes*. National Children's Bureau. London.

24. Hannon, P. (1995) *Literacy, Home and School*. Falmer. Brighton.

25. Arnold, R. (1995) *The Improvement of Schools through Partnership: School, LEA and University*. NFER. Slough

26. Bastiani, J. and Wolfendale, S. (eds 1996) *Home-School Work in Britain: Review, reflection and development*. David Fulton. London; Wolfendale, S. (1992) *Empowering Parents and Teachers: Working for children*. Cassell. London; Widlake, P. and MacLeod,

F. (1984) *Raising Standards: Parental involvement programmes and the language of children.* CEDC. Coventry.

27. Warnock, M. (1978) *Special Educational Needs: Report of the Committee of Inquiry into the education of handicapped children and young people.* HMSO. London.

28. Hancock, R. (1997) 'We need to support a fragile movement' in *Parenting Forum Newsletter.*

29. Woodhead, C. (1997) *The Guardian/Institute of Education Debate,* University of London.

30. Bastiani, J. (1997) *Home-School Work in Multi-Cultural Settings.* David Fulton. London.

31. For example, BBC Children in Need Trust.

32. From 'Headteacher's Report' in *Introductory Pack* (1997) Schools Outreach. Bromsgrove.

33. From *Information Pack* (1997) National Pyramid Trust. London.

34. Ibid.

35. Dryfoos, J. G. (1994) *Full Service Schools: A revolution in health and social services for children, youth and families.* Jossey-Bass. San Francisco.

36. From *Children's Service Plan 1997-2000.* Manchester City Council/Manchester Health Authority.

37. From McGrath, C. and Handforth, S. (1997) *Championing Children. Pilot Projects: A locally-based inter-agency approach to providing support for families.* Manchester City Council/National Children's Bureau.

38. Ibid.

39. For example, Bronfenbrenner, U. et al. (1984) 'Child, family and community' in *The Family.* University of Chicago Press.

40. Hillman, M. (1990) *One False Move.* Policy Studies Institute. London

41. SCVO (1997) *Accreditation and Vetting* in *Focus on Fact.*

42. Arnold, R. (1994) *Rural Primary Schools.* NFER. Slough.

43. See 20 above.

44. DfEE (1997) *Innovation in Drug Education: Drug education in schools.* London.

45. Hurry, J. and Lloyd, C. (1997) 'A follow-up evaluation of Project Charlie'. *Home Office Prevention Initiative. Paper* 16. Home Office. London.

46. Hand, J. (1995) *Raising Standards in Schools: The youth work contribution.* Youth Work Press, National Youth Agency. Leicester.

47. Jeffs, T. and Smith, M. (1991) 'Fallacy: the school is a poor base for youth work' in *The Charnwood Papers: Fallacies in community education* (ed. O'Hagan, R.) Education Now. Derby.

48. Jeffs, T. and Smith, M. (1996) *Informal Education: Conversation, democracy and learning.* Education Now/YMCA George Williams College. Derby.

49. Ibid.

50. Childline (1996) *Stressed Out.* London.

51. DfEE. *Permanent Exclusions from Schools in England.* Press Notice. 30 October 1997.

52. Wiltshire County Council (1996) *Children's Services Plan.*

53. Buchanan, J. (1996) Presentation at the launch of the Cambridgeshire Youth Action Scheme.

54. Ibid.

55. Utting, D. (1996) 'Reducing criminality among young people: a sample of relevant programmes in the UK'. *Home Office Research Paper* 161. Home Office. London.

56. See 40 above.

57. Cities in Schools (1996) *Annual Review.* Cambridge.

58. Ibid.

59. Ibid.

60. See, for example, 'It's not skills we lack, it's attitude', Dominic Cadbury in *Times Educational Supplement* Business Links Edition, June 1997.

61. Department of Health (1994) *Sometimes I think I Can't Go On Any More.* Health of the Nation. Department of Health.

62. Department of Health (1995) *Can Children and Young People Have Mental Health problems?* Health of the Nation. Department of Health.

63. Anderson, S. et al. (1991) *Cautionary Tales: A study of young people and crime in Edinburgh.* Centre for Criminology. University of Edinburgh.

64. Bottoms, A. (1992) 'The Community' in *Family, School and Community: Towards a social crime prevention agenda.* Crime Concern. Swindon.

65. Whitney, I. and Smith, P. K. (1993) 'A survey of the nature and extent of bully/victim problems in junior, middle and secondary schools' in *Educational Research* 35, pp. 3-25.

66. Ferguson, T. (1996) *Safe School Initiative.* Canterbury and Thanet Inter-Agency Support Group.

67. Lloyd, N. (1997) *How to Link the Prudential Youth Action Initiative with the School Curriculum.* Prudential/Crime Concern. Swindon.

68. EMU Promoting School Project *Annual Journal 1996-97.* University of Ulster. Londonderry.

69. Musgrave, R., (1998) 'Creative conflict resolution: A workshop approach in schools' in Greenwood, A. (ed.) *Taking Children Seriously.* Collins Longman.

70. From *Healthnet* (1998) the Newsletter of the European Network of Health Promoting Schools. Health Education Authority. London.

71. Health Education Authority (1993) *A Survey of Health Education Policies in Schools.* HEA. London.

72. Interview with school nurse, Paddy Jones, Epsom.

73. Crouch, V. unpublished article.

74. Anderson, S. (1997) 'Sex education and boys: a missed opportunity?' in *Health Visitor*, October, pp. 390 - 391.

75. Rowe, A. (1997) *Young People: The solution to young people's problems.* CSV. London.

76. See 37 above.

77. Shiner, M. and Newburn, T. 'Young people, drugs and peer education: an evaluation of the Youth Awareness Programme (YAP)'. *Home Office Drugs Prevention Initiative. Paper* 13. Home Office. London.

78. Kids Clubs Network *Out of School - In School!* (1994) London. Out of School Childcare Service.

79. Letter to schools from Mrs A Rumbold, Minister of State for Education, October 1989.

80. The Prince's Trust-Action *Breakthrough to Success - Study Support: A review* (1997) The Prince's Trust.

81. From *Partnership Points,* newsletter of Education/Business Partnerships, Spring 1997. Business in the Community.

82. MacBeath, J. (forthcoming) *A Place for Success: An evaluation of Study Support in England, Scotland and Northern Ireland.* The Prince's Trust. London.

83. Trust for London and City Parochial Foundation *Grants Review* 1996.

84. Interview with Mohammed Abdelrazak, Director, Resource Unit for Supplementary and Mother Tongue Schools.

85. Tower Hamlets Summer University *A Cool Move for a Hot Summer.* Published on the World Wide Web.

86. Barber, M. et al. (1997) *School Performance and Extra-Curricular Provision,* DfEE.

87. Extra Time *Newsletter, Education Extra* 1996 and 1997.

88. Northern Ireland Sports Council *Youth Sport Newletters.*

89. DfEE (1996) *Survey of School/Business Links in 1995 - DfEE Statistical Bulletin 3/96.* HMSO. London.

90. CBI (1997) *Survey of Employers' Views of School Leavers and Graduate Recruits,* CBI.

91. DES (1992) *Support for Schools: A guide to tax relief on business gifts, charitable giving and other means of support.* DES.

92. Miller, A. et al. (1995)*Making Education Our Business: Improving the quality of business-education links.* University of Warwick.

93. Ibid.

94. London Enterprise Agency (1997) *Pathways Toward Adult Life.* LENTA

95. Ibid.

96. Arnold, R. (1997) *Raising Levels of Achievement in Boys.* NFER. Slough.

97. School Curriculum and Assessment Authority/CSV *Draft Guidelines for Community Partnerships.* Unpublished.

98. CSV (1997) *Barclays New Futures: the story so far.* CSV. London.

99. Groves, M. (1980) *Community Service and the Secondary School.* NYB. Leicester.

100. Groundwork (1997) *Old Problems, Young Solutions.* Groundwork. Birmingham.

101. Ibid.

102. Lockwood, S. (1997) *Planning for Real as an Educational Resource: a project progress report.* Neighbourhood Initiatives Foundation. Telford.

103. Willow, C. (1997) *Hear! Hear! Promoting children and young people's democratic participation in local government.* Local Government Information Unit. London.

104. Ibid.

105. Citizenship Foundation. *Annual Report 1995-96.*

106. See, for example, Groundwork's publicity for the Energy Efficiency Scheme.

107. Poster, C. and Kruger, A. (1990) *Community Education in the Western World.* Routledge. London.

108. From presentation by Jean Gledhill, Headteacher, North Manchester School for Girls, at CEA/CEDC conference on the community school, November 1997.

109. From presentation by Bill Jordan, Headteacher, Dyer House School, Hartlepool, at the same conference.

110. Marriott, P. (1997) 'The role of community buildings', *Housing Research Findings* No. 218. Joseph Rowntree Foundation. York.

111. Henderson, A. (1994) *A New Generation of Evidence: the family is critical to student achievement*, Centre for Law and Education. Washington.

112. See, for example, Moss, P., and Petrie, P. (1997) *Children's Services: Time for a New Approach.* Institute of Education, University of London.